PRAISE FOR *CORSICANA*

"Arbery writes the dialogue between Ginny and Christopher, however ringed by sadness, with a sweet, intimate ease. Even moments of consternation feel amiable and well worn . . . Lot's work is a 'one way street to God,' he says. He's got no interest in money or worldly success. He bristles at the outer world thinking of people like him and Ginny as 'simple'—no, their lives are shot through with strong yearnings, deep and knowable, as undeniable but ungraspable as the light that kindles their eyes."

—VINSON CUNNINGHAM, *NEW YORKER*

"A Texas gothic about disability and small-town intolerance."

—DAVID COTE, *4COLUMNS*

"In *Corsicana*, Arbery has returned to a desaturated Texas setting with the same sense of psychological displacement; again he is writing about his own sister (though a different one) and, to some extent, his own mind. The autobiography in both adds a secret depth and ballast . . . His writing here is exquisitely judged and particular."

—HELEN SHAW, *VULTURE*

"The play is about the everyday and about everything, its lines shifting suddenly into hyperdrive, the way Will does so well, between the absolutely ordinary moment and the dizzying kaleidoscope of the rest: the world is a boop on the nose, the router not working, a dream where the bodies of the dead are standing in circles, an iPad from your dead mother, a two-liter Sprite returned to HEB, the impossible and beautiful requirement to love someone every minute and the constant failure to actually do it and the opening of your life up to some shattering revelation and the offering of every work of your hands up to God or whoever will have it."

—JIA TOLENTINO, *ALMANAC*

"*Corsicana* is not a play 'about' art, or about disability, or about race, or about giving, though all these things are present in the dramatic and intellectual tension of the work. Arbery does not offer the audience these frameworks of 'aboutness' because he is writing about people who are not 'about' one thing or even several things. He cuts off all the routes by which we might escape into ideas and avoid confronting persons . . . It's not so much that the play is a world unto itself as that each of its characters is."

—DANIEL WALDEN, *COMMONWEAL*

"Bravely, *Corsicana* is a play that acknowledges the agency and sexual desires of people that still exist in the popular imagination as helpless and sexless—accessories to one's altruism rather than complete and dynamic human beings. With its embrace of the wonderous and unknown, *Corsicana* makes one thing clear: It's okay to not have all the answers."

—ZACHARY STEWART, *THEATERMANIA*

"We are witnessing a small story with cosmic reach . . . *Corsicana* asks us to accept that the space-time continuum is just a bit fluid, with What Was, What Is, and What Will Be existing in a sort of triple exposure. Somehow it is exactly this willingness (by both playwright and characters) to step outside the confines of linear time and visible reality that make the play seem larger than its story. By the time we hear the song that Lot and Ginny have created (after much travail), there is a strange sense we have unexpectedly stumbled onto sacred ground."

—KATE FARRINGTON, *ONSTAGE NTX*

"Funny, poignant, and unsettling, *Evanston* is a formidable show that examines perceptions and delves into the spheres of the absurd and surreal."

"*Evanston Salt Costs Climbing* is funny, subtle, and deeply moving with spare, punchy dialogue à la Samuel Beckett in a Sam Shepherd-esque, classic American setting. Arbery adds unusual insight into the way human beings work together to deny reality and still love one another . . . This tiny play about love and loss and betrayal in a dying Middle America is something everyone should see and then talk about."

"*Evanston* follows the angst-filled trajectory of two sad-eyed salt truck drivers . . . If you spread salt for a living, the play posits, that dread flows from one of the play's main themes: the clash between our collective responsibility to the planet and the economic fate of individuals."

"In Will Arbery's strange and wonderful play *Evanston Salt Costs Climbing*, the impending doom of climate change, economic precariousness, and urban decay are not merely abstract concerns. They are dark and stultifying forces that can make even time go out of whack. Set over three Januarys in 2014, 2015, and 2016, the play contains elements of Harold Pinter's existential foreboding, Edward Albee's quotidian absurdism, and Annie Baker's linguistic loopiness. Yet, in Arbery's work these all seem fresh and new . . . In drawing out the humor in life's ridiculousness, *Evanston* is oddly and refreshingly affirming."

"*Evanston Salt Costs Climbing* is a song for the striving: a love letter to those who feel too much, who can't help but give and give of themselves even if it comes at their own expense."

CORSICANA

EVANSTON SALT COSTS CLIMBING

OTHER BOOKS BY WILL ARBERY PUBLISHED BY TCG

Heroes of the Fourth Turning

CORSICANA

EVANSTON SALT COSTS CLIMBING

Will Arbery

THEATRE COMMUNICATIONS GROUP / NEW YORK / 2024

Due to space constraints, credit information for quoted material is detailed on page 185.

The publication of *Corsicana/Evanston Salt Costs Climbing* by Will Arbery, through TCG Books, is made possible with support by Mellon Foundation.

TCG books are exclusively distributed to the book trade by Consortium Book Sales and Distribution.

Library of Congress Control Numbers:
2023044460 (print) / 2023044461 (ebook)
ISBN 978-1-63670-186-8 (paperback) / ISBN 978-1-63670-187-5 (ebook)
A catalog record for this book is available from the Library of Congress.

Book design and composition by Lisa Govan
Cover design by Mark Melnick
Cover art by Deirdre O'Connell

First Edition, March 2024

CONTENTS

CORSICANA

For Julia

Thank you first and foremost to Sam Gold. This impossible thing happened because of you. Thank you to Amy and Jo. A bottomless thank you to Frances Gold. And thank you to the incredible cast, Will Dagger, Harold Surratt, Didi O'Connell, and Jamie Brewer. This play *was* you. Thank you Isabella Byrd, Justin Ellington, Lacl Jellinek, Cate McCrea, Amanda Spooner, Ryan Dobrin, Zach Brecheen, Andie Burns, Joshua Yocom, Ilene Reid, Gigi Buffington and Qween Jean. Huge thank you to Joanna Sternberg for the gift of your beautiful songs. Thank you Adam Greenfield and Natasha Sinha and Lizzie Stern and Billy McEntee and Blake Zidell and Playwrights Horizons. Thank you Tom Park and David Skinner for your initial support in writing this play. Thank you to Greg Nobile for getting it over the finish line. Thank you to Brian D. Coats, Elizabeth Kenny, Ansa Akyea, K. Todd Freeman, and especially Lauren Potter. Thank you to John MacGregor, Olivier Sultan, Eva Dickerman, Lewis Hyde, Kyle Hobratschk, David Searcy, Nancy Rebal, Wayne Hall, 100W Corsicana, Sam Barickman, Di Glazer, Jacob Robinson, Abigail Friedman, Loddie Allison, Chloé Cooper Jones, Jia Tolentino, Emily Davis, and Ryan Haddad. Thank you to Robert Egan, Mark Seldis, Jose Delgado, Ramon Valdez, Stephen Tyler Howell, and Adam O'Byrne. Thank you to the Ojai Playwrights Conference and Interstate 73. Thank you to Gavin Morrison and Lucia Simek. Special thank you to Joan Arbery and Glenn Arbery and Virginia Arbery. Hi Yi. Love you. Thanks Hilary Duff! Thank you, most especially, to the unstoppable Julia "Joofbox" Arbery, to whom this play is totally & completely dedicated. Pop goes my heart.

PRODUCTION HISTORY

Corsicana had its world premiere at Playwrights Horizons (Adam Greenfield, Artistic Director; Leslie Marcus, Managing Director) in New York City on June 22, 2022, produced by special arrangement with Seaview Productions. It was directed by Sam Gold. The set design was by Lael Jellinek and Cate McCrea, the costume design was by Qween Jean, the lighting design was by Isabella Byrd, the sound design was by Justin Ellington, the music direction was by Ilene Reid, the music composition was by Joanna Sternberg; the voice and text coach was Gigi Buffington, the production stage manager was Amanda Spooner. The cast was:

GINNY	Jamie Brewer
CHRISTOPHER	Will Dagger
JUSTICE	Deirdre O'Connell
LOT	Harold Surratt

Corsicana was developed at Playwrights Horizons; at Page 73 (Michael Walkup, Artistic Director), as part of their Interstate 73 Writers Group; and at the 2021 Ojai Playwrights Conference (Robert Egan, Producing Artistic Director; Mark Seldis, Managing Director). *Corsicana* was originally commissioned by Shadowcatcher Entertainment.

CHARACTERS

GINNY, female, white, a woman with Down syndrome, a volunteer, a singer, thirty-four

CHRISTOPHER, male, white, Ginny's half-brother, a film teacher at the community college, thirty-three

JUSTICE, female, white, Lot's best friend, Ginny and Christopher's honorary aunt, a writer, late sixties

LOT, male, Black, an artist, a musician, sixties

SETTING

Early summer, 2022. Two spaces in Corsicana, Texas:

Lot's house—a bare-bones space in the middle of nowhere, full of art that we never see.

Ginny's house—one-story, ranch-style, doesn't get great light.

When you give a gift there is momentum, and the weight shifts from body to body . . .
The gift moves in a circle . . .
The gift leaves all boundary and circles into mystery . . .

—Lewis Hyde, *The Gift*

You just have to say it out loud.

—Julia Arbery

Part One

Christopher and Ginny's house, which used to be their mom's house: a dusty little Texas ranch-style. Christopher is in the den on his phone and Ginny comes over and looks at him.

He eventually looks up from his phone and touches her nose.

CHRISTOPHER: Boop.
GINNY: Haha. So.

(He notices that she's upset.)

CHRISTOPHER: Are you okay?
GINNY: I'm not sure.
CHRISTOPHER: What's wrong?
GINNY: I'm not sure. Big hug?
CHRISTOPHER: Yeah.

(He gives her a big hug. She cries into his arms. Or maybe she wants to cry but can't.)

Oh no. Okay. It's okay.

(This happens for a while. And then she pulls away.)

GINNY: I need to do something.
CHRISTOPHER: You need to do something?
GINNY: I need you to help me do something.
CHRISTOPHER: Like what?
GINNY: Something to do.

(She looks at the ground.)

I don't have anything to do.
CHRISTOPHER: Are you bored?
GINNY: No. I'm worried. I can't find my heart.
CHRISTOPHER: Oh. You can't find your heart. Okay—
GINNY: I can't feel anything there.
CHRISTOPHER: Oh no. Okay, so let's get active again. Let's get your job back at the nursing home.
GINNY: No.
CHRISTOPHER: No? What about the choir?
GINNY: No.
CHRISTOPHER: Why not?
GINNY: I don't belong.
CHRISTOPHER: Yes you do. Everyone loves you.
GINNY: Not if I'm not happy.
CHRISTOPHER: They always love you.
GINNY: Not if I'm not like me.
CHRISTOPHER: You don't feel like you?
GINNY: No.
CHRISTOPHER: Oh, man.
GINNY: But that's okay.
CHRISTOPHER: No, it's not. Okay, let's . . .

(He gets out his phone and starts filming her.)

GINNY: What are you doing?

CHRISTOPHER: Say something to your friends. We'll send it to Tim and Angelo and Justice.

GINNY: What do you want me to say?

CHRISTOPHER: Whatever you want. Something funny.

(Pause.)

GINNY *(To the camera)*: Hi, everyone. This is Ginny. I miss you but I need space. I'm not feeling good.

(She covers her face.)

I hate this.

CHRISTOPHER *(Still filming)*: Okay just shake it loose. Ginny. HONK! GINNY! What do you wanna say to your BOYS!

(She doesn't show her face. He keeps trying. He tries to get the camera in her face to make her laugh, and she pushes it away. He stops filming.)

Sorry.

GINNY: It's okay.

CHRISTOPHER: I'm sorry, Ginny.

GINNY: It's not a big deal.

CHRISTOPHER: No, it is. Have I been—

GINNY: Have you been what?

CHRISTOPHER: Just kind of. Asleep.

GINNY: No you're awake.

CHRISTOPHER: No I'm so . . .

GINNY: I'm just not in the mood.

CHRISTOPHER: Yeah.

GINNY: Because I'm lazy.

CHRISTOPHER: No you're not. I am.

GINNY: Yeah you are.

CHRISTOPHER: You think I'm lazy?

GINNY: Just a little bit.

CHRISTOPHER: Yeah we're just . . . Okay. We need to—we're just, like, little kids. We don't know what to do. Like we're waiting for her to come in and just be like, *let's eat, let's go to church, let's* . . . but we're just little kids.

GINNY: No, we're adults.

CHRISTOPHER: You're right.

GINNY: I'm thirty-four years old and you're thirty-three years old.

CHRISTOPHER: You're right.

GINNY: So we have to be adults.

CHRISTOPHER: Okay.

GINNY: So you have to figure that out.

CHRISTOPHER: Okay I get it.

GINNY: And shave your face.

CHRISTOPHER: What? No.

GINNY: Are you sure?

CHRISTOPHER: You don't like the mustache?

GINNY: No. But I'm open-minded, actually. So be yourself.

CHRISTOPHER: Okay . . .

GINNY: I can help you to be yourself. I need you to help me to be myself. And that's hard for me to say, because I don't like asking for help.

CHRISTOPHER: Okay. I understand. And I'm sorry for being lazy and scared.

GINNY: That's fine.

CHRISTOPHER: Okay. I'm gonna—okay.

(*Now:*

Justice is unloading groceries in their kitchen. Christopher enters in his sleep clothes.)

JUSTICE: Oh, sorry!

CHRISTOPHER: What are you—

JUSTICE: Nothing to see here.

CHRISTOPHER: You didn't have to do that.

JUSTICE: Just a few things. I was already there.

CHRISTOPHER: Oh man thanks, Justice. Thanks. Yeah sorry—I think I took on too many classes.

(He holds up some Sprite.)

Oh thanks. Oh is this for Ginny?

JUSTICE: She asked for it directly.

CHRISTOPHER: I'm trying to get her off soda. Is that dumb?

JUSTICE: No that's probably very not dumb. Should I take it back?

CHRISTOPHER: Yeah maybe. Is that okay?

JUSTICE: Sure, I'll give it to the church. Or I like Sprite.

CHRISTOPHER: I just think it's not good for her. I don't know. Whatever I don't know.

JUSTICE: Did you talk to her about it?

CHRISTOPHER: I tried. No, I don't know. I just thought I'd wean her off it slowly. Like be a better influence. It's dumb it's manipulative. I just want her to feel better.

JUSTICE: And you?

CHRISTOPHER: Me? No, I eat terribly, I'm a huge hypocrite.

JUSTICE: No, how are *you* feeling?

CHRISTOPHER: Oh. I mean who can say.

JUSTICE: Uh-huh.

CHRISTOPHER: What about you?

JUSTICE: Heavy. Slow to joy. Missing your mom. More than I know what to do with.

CHRISTOPHER: Yeah. It's.

JUSTICE: Yeah. Don't know where to put it all.

CHRISTOPHER: Yeah, exactly. It's.

(Pause.)

Sorry. It's hard for me to, uh—

JUSTICE: Don't be sorry.

CHRISTOPHER: Ginny said I'm lazy.

JUSTICE: You're not lazy.

CHRISTOPHER: I think I am. I know I am. H-E-B is literally on the way home from work, it's right there, I could just go in and get groceries and I don't. I don't make things better. And what am I, the king of dust?

JUSTICE: Ha! Well there's a writer I love who calls dust "matter in the wrong place." And laziness "temperament not aligning with environment." Shut up, Justice. I thought we had a plan, Christopher. I thought you liked that idea of going to see Lot.

CHRISTOPHER: Yeah I did like that idea. I'm just nervous. But let's do it.

JUSTICE: No I'm not coming with you.

CHRISTOPHER: Really?

JUSTICE: No he won't talk to you if I'm there. He's too used to me. He'll answer all your questions right to my face.

CHRISTOPHER: Is he mean?

JUSTICE: Nahhh.

CHRISTOPHER: Okay. Okay I'll go. I'm just nervous. I mean it feels weird to just show up and—but it's the best idea we've got and I'm gonna go I'm just nervous.

JUSTICE: No, don't be nervous. Look, you drive that long road and it feels like nothing at first. And then suddenly it's just something. And it's great. He's great. Something's shifted in him lately. He's letting himself be seen. And letting me spend whole days with him, and it's been . . . it's really been—well. Who knows. You're gonna love him, Christopher. I have a good feeling about it.

CHRISTOPHER: That's good.

JUSTICE: Just see how it feels.

CHRISTOPHER: Okay.

JUSTICE: I have a good feeling about it.

CHRISTOPHER: Do you?

JUSTICE: Sort of a dream.

CHRISTOPHER: Yeah. What?

JUSTICE: Like a dream. Like I dreamt it. Like I dreamt it already happened and it went great. Don't know if I really did dream it, all I can remember for sure from my dreams lately is circles, circles of bodies, standing, bodies of the dead standing in circles. But not in a bad way. And this feels part of that. So I feel good. Like I know what's gonna happen already, even though I don't know, and it's good, and I'm just impatient to get to that goodness. And it's *very* selfish. Like good things come out of it for me. I feel implicated. But first you gotta go do your thing. Then I'll know what my thing is. But no rush, I can wait. And I might be wrong about all this. I'm just meddlesome. I'm just guessing.

(*Now:*

   Christopher steps into Lot's small house, which is full of art and some trash that will soon be art. But we don't see any of it.)

CHRISTOPHER: Hello . . . ?

LOT (*Off*): What. Dangit. Who—uh—oh—I'm not wearing pants— Who is that—

CHRISTOPHER: It's uh—

LOT (*Off*): I'm not wearing pants—

CHRISTOPHER: Sorry!

LOT (*Off*): Who uh—one moment.

(*Lot emerges from his secret workspace. He's wearing pants.*)

Who's that?

CHRISTOPHER: Hi, sorry. I would have called but—

LOT: Yeah no telephone—

CHRISTOPHER: Yeah of course, so I'm sorry for— So—so—

LOT: You saw that article? Is that all happening now?

CHRISTOPHER: Oh, no I—do you remember—no, Justice introduced us, we met in the street fair, last month. We talked
about uh, I was the one you played that song for—

LOT: Oh.

CHRISTOPHER: Do you remember? That beautiful song?

LOT: I played it?

CHRISTOPHER: Yeah by the—by Justice's book sale . . . Justice is
a friend of my family's.

LOT: Justice is a friend of everyone's family.

CHRISTOPHER: That's true. But she's like really sort of a part of
mine.

LOT: Well me too. So?

CHRISTOPHER: Oh but anyway—

LOT: Which song?

CHRISTOPHER: Oh, it was, it was beautiful. I think it was called
"Weird."

LOT: Yeah, oh yeah, yeah, "Weird." I remember you. I played
you "Weird."

CHRISTOPHER: Yeah, I loved it. I'm sorry for just showing up,
I just didn't know—

LOT: It's fine.

CHRISTOPHER: Oh good yeah Justice said to just show up, so—

LOT: Yeah that's fine—the gate's open at the front, that means
you're welcome. I keep it open now. Visitors welcome.

CHRISTOPHER: Great, good—

LOT: Anyway I was ready. There's been a question in the air
lately.

CHRISTOPHER: Oh yeah?

LOT: Yeah so I didn't know what to expect with a question in the
air—so I've been working hard and just working hard and

harder—getting weird and working hard—so I didn't know what to expect—when there's a question like that in the air.

CHRISTOPHER: What—uh—sorry what question?

LOT: About whether people'd be showing up. I was grieving but it was closing me up. Now I want the grieving to open me up. And I opened my heart up and then the article happened.

CHRISTOPHER: Oh I'm sorry to hear you've been grieving. I am too.

LOT: That's okay.

CHRISTOPHER: Yeah. Well—yeah Justice showed me that article in *Oxford American* and it was really so good. Like so cool. So so cool. It really made me proud to be from Corsicana. And the whole layout, the spread, the art looked so good, it was so cool and so fancy. And yeah just congratulations and yeah just like what's it like to be so fancy?

LOT: Is it so absurd that The Fancy and I could commingle?

CHRISTOPHER: Oh not at all, sorry if I . . . oh wait I recognize some of these guys! This is the same art here that was in the—it's right here!

LOT: Some of it. The rest she took away in a box.

CHRISTOPHER: Oh cool, to show it? That's awesome.

LOT: You're enthusiastic.

CHRISTOPHER: I am?

LOT: The word "enthusiasm" means "possessed by God."

CHRISTOPHER: Oh, cool. How'd this writer find you?

LOT: It's all Justice's fault. Some friend of Justice, some friend from Dallas who saw my things. She came down, poked around, saw what I'd—yeah. And I guess she—yeah. She had a lot of ideas about what it all meant. And she wrote down the ideas and came back down and we went through it together. With a pen. And some of it felt okay to me.

CHRISTOPHER: Really special.

LOT: Not *special*.

CHRISTOPHER: What?

LOT: Not *special*.

> It's not *special*.
>
> It just *is*.
>
> Not *special* it just *is*.

CHRISTOPHER: Right. Sorry.

LOT: Well she has whole books full of that kind of thinking. I fit into some vision she had of the world and what's beautiful in it.

CHRISTOPHER: Yeah I mean I wish I fit into someone's uh—

LOT: Why are you here?

CHRISTOPHER: Okay right uh—my name is Christopher and I was wondering if you'd want to um—if you were in the position to—like if you were looking for— I was wondering if I could give you a little work?

LOT: Your work?

CHRISTOPHER: What?

LOT: Work you made? You want to give it to me?

CHRISTOPHER: Oh—no—what I meant was I was wondering if I could, like, *employ* you. Like a part-time gig thing—just like if you're not too busy.

LOT: What kinda work?

CHRISTOPHER: Well—yeah! I know you're getting all famous for your sculptures but it's, uh, it's actually about your music. You're such a multi-hyphenate, it's intimidating.

LOT: I'm a what?

CHRISTOPHER: Just—I thought your song was really beautiful, obviously—and I wonder if you'd want to collaborate with my sister? Musically? Or just spend some time?

LOT: Your sister? Spend some time—

CHRISTOPHER: Sure, yeah, just spend some time, and maybe make things together—or get her in the making mood— get her making . . . I could pay you, to help her get creative?

LOT: Get creative?

CHRISTOPHER: She loves music—she really loves music.

LOT: Okay.

CHRISTOPHER: And I'm sure you two have wildly different taste, but—maybe you could help her make some music.

LOT: Like lessons?

CHRISTOPHER: If you want!

LOT: Or what?

CHRISTOPHER: Lessons—or just, just hanging out—while I'm at work? Or—making a song together.

LOT: Is it hanging out or is it making something?

CHRISTOPHER: I think making a song?

LOT: Just one song?

CHRISTOPHER: Yeah I mean I think one song would feel momentous. Like for her to say, "Look I made this." She's a natural performer. And then maybe I could make a music video for the song. I make— I mean I work at the community college—I teach film.

LOT: At Navarro?

CHRISTOPHER: Yeah, I used to teach in Dallas, actually—well, Denton. I was making more stuff there. We had a production company. My friend and I. "Elbow Productions." It's an inside joke.

LOT: Okay.

CHRISTOPHER: I met him at UNT. Yeah he might come down and we might make something. Like a horror. This town would be great for a horror. But it's hard. There's *some* film stuff happening here—well not Corsicana but Dallas— greater Dallas—the metroplex—but you know, not like LA. Plus I fell out with some of those guys. Even before I had to move down here.

LOT: Why are you telling me the novel of you?

CHRISTOPHER: Oh sorry! Different art scenes I guess. I mean yeah—Ginny just needs something to do. Yeah our mom passed away last Christmas and she—yeah they were like *this*. And now she doesn't have her buddy. And neither of our dads are in the picture. And she's—she's grieving, she's . . . uh. I've never seen her like this and I want to get her brain, uh—or just—get her social—give her some structure.

LOT: Sounds like babysitting.

CHRISTOPHER: It's not—no—that's not what this is. It's *artistic*.

LOT: Is this something she wants to do?

CHRISTOPHER: I think so, I think she'd enjoy it.

LOT: How old is she?

CHRISTOPHER: She's thirty-four.

LOT *(After a beat)*: Why do you want me to babysit your grown-ass sister?

CHRISTOPHER: No! Oh—sorry. I didn't explain. She has Down syndrome. It's not babysitting, and please, don't call it that around her. But she has—yeah, she has Down syndrome.

(Lot nods. Spits.)

LOT: "Special needs."

CHRISTOPHER: Right, yeah.

LOT: Yeah I know "special needs." Why'd you come here? I know the place in the high school. The hallway in the high school. You know I'm not one of them, right?

CHRISTOPHER: What?

LOT: I'm not special needs.

CHRISTOPHER: Oh—I didn't think you were. I assumed the opposite.

LOT: What's the opposite? I was only a couple years in that hall-way. And they knew I didn't belong. Got a graduate degree in my forties. So don't worry about me.

CHRISTOPHER: Oh, cool. In what?

LOT: Experimental mathematics. I proved the existence of God.

CHRISTOPHER: Are you serious? Can I see?

LOT: I threw it away. Art's a better delivery system. It's Down syndrome?

CHRISTOPHER: Yeah.

LOT: And it's about making a song that's hers.

CHRISTOPHER: A song that's hers. Yeah. Like how cool would that be.

LOT: I never did anything like this. This isn't what I was expecting at all.

CHRISTOPHER: Yeah—

LOT: Don't think I'd be good.

CHRISTOPHER: I bet you would be.

LOT: You don't know.

CHRISTOPHER: That's true—but Justice said that you're one of the best people ever, pretty much, so—

LOT: Justice is biased.

CHRISTOPHER: Maybe so.

LOT: Justice is just my friend, that's what.

CHRISTOPHER: Well she spoke very highly of you.

LOT: Justice and I, we agreed, we believe in gifts, not capital. It's a prison. To consume, to consume. And then evacuate. To toss out. It's sinful. It's man made. It's all a man-made evil.

CHRISTOPHER: Oh okay—yeah . . .

LOT: So think of a gift to give me in return. One day down the line. That's the rubric.

CHRISTOPHER: Oh really? Okay I will. I absolutely will. Does this mean you're—

LOT: Making one song with one person. Fine. Good for me if it's good for her. What's her name?

CHRISTOPHER: Her name is Ginny.

LOT: How often you thinking for Ginny?

CHRISTOPHER: Well I teach four days a week—but it could be—we could try it out slower. Yeah, something slower, to respect your time. Mondays only or something?

LOT: Mondays I could do. Let's start with Mondays or some shit.

> Hell—now I have to start knowing what day is Monday.
> Hell—now I have to get a calendar or something.
> And keep track of what day is Monday—hell.

(Now:

> *Christopher standing in the threshold, looking at Ginny.)*

CHRISTOPHER: Ginny, I made an appointment for you on Monday. With a musician. His name is Lot. He's Justice's friend. He's gonna make a song with you.

GINNY: A song?

CHRISTOPHER: Yeah. Doesn't that sound fun?

GINNY: Not really.

CHRISTOPHER: Okay. Well can you just go? He's excited to meet you. The song can be about everything you're feeling right now. I think it's good—you know? It's good, I think, to try to make something out of— I don't know. Right?

GINNY: I get it. I'll go.

CHRISTOPHER: Okay. Really? Okay cool. Thank you.

(Christopher turns to leave.)

GINNY: But I did have a nightmare that you ran away.

CHRISTOPHER: What?

GINNY: Mom always loved to take me on girl dates and say that men run away. That's what they do.

CHRISTOPHER: But I'm not gonna—Ginny, I'm right here.

(Now:

> *Christopher's gone. Justice is there, eating Sonic. Ginny's singing The Chicks' song to herself.)*

GINNY *(Singing)*:
>Cowboy take me away
>Fly this girl as high as you can
>Into the wild blue
>Set me free, oh, I pray—

(The CD starts skipping: ". . . pray . . ." repeats over and over.)

OH COME ON. I HATE THIS. I HATE MYSELF.
JUSTICE: No you don't!
GINNY: Is that Justice?
JUSTICE: Yes!

(Ginny appears.)

GINNY: Why are you here?
JUSTICE: I'm babysitting you!
GINNY: I'M AN ADULT.

(Ginny storms off.)

I NEED SOME SPACE.
JUSTICE: YOU'RE RIGHT! I APOLOGIZE.
>*(To herself:)* Come on, Justice.

(Now:
>*Justice is in Lot's space. He's mixing glue.)*

JUSTICE: I tell you what happened with the dead man? I was getting ready for a bash, some donor for the library was throwing some kinda bash?
LOT: Is this a dream?
JUSTICE: No—not a dream.
LOT: Real life?
JUSTICE: I don't know—maybe. I guess so.

LOT: You're weird.

JUSTICE: Whatever. So I was looking in the mirror like *how much am I gonna wanna dance tonight, how much am I gonna wanna be moving around?* And then back behind me in the mirror suddenly it's a man holding out a dress for me. Yeah. And what's funny is that at first I'm like—*hell that's my only dress, nah, pick something else, I haven't worn that since my forties, I don't wear a dress unless forced*— I think maybe even I say that out loud before I realize, like, okay, um *what!* There's a man in my room! And then I turn around and he's not there of course.

LOT: Is this real?

JUSTICE: Let me finish.

LOT: You're weird.

JUSTICE: But what's interesting is in that moment upon real-izing his presence, I felt like I knew exactly who he was in my life. He was someone very specific to me, someone I was used to having around. And now for the life of me I can't remember who he was, to me, in that moment—but the *feeling*, the comfort of being with him, felt like it had a full *lifetime* of evidence behind it.

LOT: Who was it?

JUSTICE: Shut up!

LOT: I just think you're weird. I just don't know why you're not telling me if this is real or not.

JUSTICE: It's real. Okay? It's real—everything's real. It's all real to me. You're the one who showed me how to pay closer attention to these things. So shut up.

So. It wasn't the *seeing* of him that was scary, it was the *forgetting* of how I knew him . . . I was much more scared of my brain afterwards, than my brain during. You know?

LOT: No.

JUSTICE: And then I saw him again. *Been* seeing him around—in church, at the library, in front of my headlights at night—

and every time it's like a prayer when you really get inside it—a sort of cave you get into, or a bubble floating in space, for a few minutes you get inside a bubble, which is its own world unto itself, nothing getting in or out, except *you* get in, and *you* get out—but you can't remember what it was like inside there. You know?

LOT: . . . yeah. *That* I know.

JUSTICE: I know. *That* you know. It's a funny feeling. You know that you went *in* there, and you know that you feel different *now*, but you don't know how you felt *then*.

That's what's started happening with this dead man. Makes it non-catastrophic, somehow. He's scary as hell, but he doesn't have power. I can fear him and want him at the same time. I can love how he makes me feel, and not *know* how he makes me feel, all at the same time. I just look forward to seeing him because I know I'm gonna feel *some* type of way. And then when he's gone I can't remember how it was that I felt. Only that I'm breathing slower and my spine is numb.

LOT: Could be a vitamin deficiency. Maybe you just need to eat more fish.

JUSTICE: Shut up. I saw him out on my lawn though yesterday which is why it's forefront in my mind. He was interrogating the air. I don't know how else to put it—he had the air around us pinned down and he was interrogating it. Which I think made me feel interrogated as well. Something was wanted from me, in a way it hadn't been before. I was pulled to the earth fast. Knees first. Skinned my knees.

(She pulls up her pants and examines her skinned knees. Lot looks at them.)

LOT: You okay?

JUSTICE: I'm okay, of course.

LOT: You can't remember how you know him?

JUSTICE: Who said I know him?

LOT: I thought you did.

JUSTICE: No I don't know that for sure. Or whether it's *me* who's doing the knowing. Might be that someone else takes over, in those moments, and *they're* the one who knows him. I dunno.

LOT: But you feel okay with him.

JUSTICE: So far. Learning as I go.

LOT: I just don't want him to switch all the sudden and get angry.

JUSTICE: I don't see that happening.

LOT: Well.

JUSTICE: Well, we'll see.

LOT: We will.

(Lot goes back into his secret workspace.)

I'm gonna start a new job soon I guess.

JUSTICE: What's that?

LOT *(Off)*: I think you might be responsible.

JUSTICE: How so?

LOT *(Off)*: You told some guy that I was trustworthy.

JUSTICE: I did?

LOT *(Off)*: Some guy from Navarro, he's got a special sister.

JUSTICE: Oh yeah, that guy, yeah he was asking after you.

(Lot comes back out.)

LOT: You don't have to lie.

JUSTICE: About what?

LOT: I know he's like family to you, not just some guy.

JUSTICE: Yeah okay whatever. I just didn't want you to think I was pulling strings.

LOT: Well are you?

JUSTICE: No, Christopher was asking about you!

LOT: Okay. You know I kinda struggle sometimes.

JUSTICE: I know.

LOT: I don't know what I can teach this girl.

JUSTICE: Just see where it takes you.

LOT: Okay.

JUSTICE: Big year. Getting your art out there. Meeting new people. Collaborating. You given any more thought to the idea of a little gallery showing?

LOT: Don't wanna think about that right now.

JUSTICE: Okay. Just let me know when you're ready and I'll call Gail for you.

LOT: Okay. Gotta ask though.

JUSTICE: Okay.

LOT: About this girl.

JUSTICE: Ginny, okay, yeah.

LOT: Why's he asking me to, uh—with this Down syndrome . . . does he think *I'm*—

JUSTICE: Does he think you're what?

LOT: I dunno. Sometimes I just can't tell my place in things.

JUSTICE: Your place in things is wherever you want it to be, just like anyone.

LOT: Okay. Thank you for the sermonizing.

JUSTICE: What sermonizing?

LOT: Forget it.

JUSTICE: Okay well I think I'm a haunted troll and I think you're brilliant and I think we're peas in a pod. You and I. That's all.

LOT: I've never been peas in a pod with anyone.

JUSTICE: Well I think you are with me.

LOT: I don't know about that.

JUSTICE: Forget I said it.

LOT: I will.

JUSTICE: Is she coming here?

LOT: Well I'm not going *there*.

JUSTICE: Hell you gotta clean this place up then.

LOT: What? No.

(*Now:*

Ginny is in Lot's house. They stare at each other a while before they speak.)

LOT: So what kinda things you like.

GINNY: What?

LOT: What kinda—what kinda things you like?

GINNY: Oh, I don't know.

LOT: Oh yeah?

(*Pause.*)

GINNY: I like listening to music.

LOT: Is that all you like?

GINNY: No.

LOT: Okay. What else you like?

GINNY: Lots of stuff.

LOT: Mhm.

(*Pause.*)

One thing I like is I like making things with my hands.

GINNY: Right. What things?

LOT: I make things, I don't know. I just make them.

GINNY: Yeah. I like your shirt.

LOT: What?

GINNY: I like your shirt.

LOT: I guess it's an okay shirt . . .

GINNY: Yeah.

LOT: I didn't make it.

(Ginny laughs nervously. Lot gets very uncomfortable. Ginny gets out her iPad and starts watching something.)

What are you doing?
GINNY: Watching Disney Channel.
LOT: Oh. How?
GINNY: This is my iPad from my mom.
LOT: But I don't have internet.
GINNY: We downloaded it to watch in the car.
LOT: Oh.

(Ginny watches the show. Silence. Lot goes into his secret work-space and starts working on a sculpture. Ginny gets bored and sad.)

GINNY: When is my brother coming?
LOT: I don't know. Later. This was dumb.
GINNY: I don't like that word.
LOT: Okay.
GINNY: And I don't actually know you.
LOT: That's because we've never met.

(Now:
Christopher's picking Ginny up. She's in the bathroom.)

LOT: I don't want to keep doing this.
CHRISTOPHER: Oh. No? Why not?
LOT: Just don't.
CHRISTOPHER: Oh, okay . . . that's . . . hm. Okay. Shoot. Are you sure?
LOT: She just sat there and watched something called *Jessie* for three hours. I think I'm just her babysitter. And if I'm doing that I should get paid capital just for being, uh—useless. Money is only good for useless people.

CHRISTOPHER: You're not useless. You're not a babysitter. And I could absolutely pay you if . . . look I'm sorry it didn't go well but I think you just have to get into a groove, right? She won't have her iPad next time.

LOT: Well I don't think she has much interest.

CHRISTOPHER: In what?

LOT: Anything.

CHRISTOPHER: She has a lot of interest. In a lot of things. She hasn't been herself. It's—

LOT: Nah I get the feeling that she doesn't like me.

CHRISTOPHER: Is that the issue?

LOT: Yeah.

CHRISTOPHER: Well that's easy. Ginny!

(The toilet flushes. Ginny comes out.)

GINNY: Okay, that bathroom has some monsters in it.

LOT: Those are sculptures.

GINNY: Oh that's okay.

CHRISTOPHER: Ginny do you like Lot?

GINNY: Who?

CHRISTOPHER: Lot—right here, asshole.

GINNY *(After a beat)*: Hm . . .

LOT: See? She doesn't like me.

CHRISTOPHER: Yes she *does*.

GINNY: I do.

CHRISTOPHER: She does.

GINNY: Yeah. Kind of a lot. And I want to make a song. We have to get to work and not be shy.

LOT: I'm not shy I just miss my Mondays, dangit. Fine. This is what you get. This what you get when you say okay.

(Now:
    The next Monday. Ginny has paper and pencils in front of her. She starts tapping one of the pencils.)

LOT: One thing I sometimes want to write about is how I lost my best friend.

GINNY: Oh wow.

LOT: Yeah. Her name was Mary Ellen. She lived over there. I miss her. She was my mother. She was a miracle and a maniac.

GINNY: A what?

LOT: A miracle and a maniac.

GINNY: That's awesome.

LOT: Yeah, just my best friend. She died twelve years ago.

GINNY: Oh I can't believe that. Do you want a hug?

LOT: No thanks. Can't believe he got her.

GINNY: Oh, right.

LOT: Don't you wanna know who got her?

GINNY: Who?

LOT: Well in the 1880s a one-legged man showed up in town and tightrope-walked across Main Street and fell to his death. He's buried in the cemetery not too far from my mother. Nobody knew his name, so all it says on the stone is: ROPE WALKER. He came to town and hung the rope. He told the town to watch him walk it. Then he fell. But what no one knows is: he didn't fall, he was pushed.

GINNY: Are you kidding? By who?

LOT: Dinosaur. Anyone who lives here long enough knows that there are dinosaur ghosts all around us. And they been here for a long time but they get wiser the longer they stay. Sad ghosts of dinosaurs. They can't die and they just get wiser so they just get sadder. There used to be a Ku Klux Klan group that met right in the center of town. And one time they were having a ritual and nearly burned the town down because their building set on fire. They were doing their hateful things and suddenly they all felt enormous wings flapping around them. Their candles fell and were burning their garments and banners and things. They all swore they were being attacked by what felt like a giant bat. And they had gashes on their skin to prove it. But it wasn't a bat, it was a pterodactyl. So now you know.

(Pause.)

GINNY: Your mom got eaten by a dinosaur?

LOT: Kinda. Felt like it.

GINNY: That's kinda scary.

LOT: Wanna sing about it?

GINNY: No.

LOT: Yeah, right, that was my thing. What about one of your things? Wanna sing about having Down syndrome?

GINNY: Huh? No.

LOT: Yeah.

GINNY: Or maybe so.

LOT: Okay.

GINNY: I can talk, not sing.

LOT: Okay, talk.

GINNY: Okay. So just talking? Fine. About what? Fine.

I'm not the only one who has Down syndrome. I've been this way my entire life.

It's hard for some people to understand, they don't know how to react. But it means I'm special and I have some problems—shaking problems, and a good imagination, like I can't control my body at night, and sometimes I cry and cough. And I'm healthy.

The best thing about being a woman with Down syndrome is being smart, and doing lots of special things for people, and helping old people, helping others.

I'm happy God made me how I am because I have blue eyes. And I am sensitive.

My heart is like this dream-wish about things. The best thing about my heart is that I can talk to anybody.

LOT: I think that can be a song.

GINNY: Like what?

LOT: Like:

(Singing:)

> I'm not the only one who has Down syndrome
> No, I'm not the only one who has Down syndrome—

GINNY: Okay—no.

LOT: No?

GINNY: No. No.

LOT: Okay.

GINNY: Your voice is weird.

LOT: Oh.

GINNY: I like it.

LOT: Thanks.

GINNY: I don't know. I don't want to sing about Down syndrome. Maybe my half-brother. Or my friends. Maybe my mom.

LOT: You wanna write about your mom?

GINNY: Actually, no.

LOT: Or your brother?

GINNY: Okay!

LOT: Okay.

GINNY: Christopher's a good half-brother, um . . . I don't like when he's lazy and doesn't know how to be an adult. I like when he takes me to see the movies and I wish he didn't get so upset about his students. But he has dreams about true love and I know we'll get there together.

LOT: Yeah.

GINNY: Yeah.

LOT: You wanna just sing?

You wanna just sing some of your thoughts about Christopher?

Like I'll show you. Like I'll do it about my friend Justice.
Like:

(He starts singing. It's impromptu and weird but awesome.)

Justice is a friend to me
Justice made a home for me
Justice is a friend

I needed somewhere to sleep
Needed somewhere to make a mess
Needed some place to call my own

Weird without my family
Weird with my Mama dead
My sister gone to Little Rock
Was getting weird that day
Weird before the people knew
Just who I am or what I do
No one knew a thing 'bout me
My sister gone my family dead

Justice found me a good lot
Justice said this is Lot's lot
Justice found me a good price

She went in and raised the frame
A couple boys from town they came
And lifted the house up for me

The sun was hot we drank a lot
Ozarka, Ozarka, water jug,
Distilled Ozarka

Justice! Oh Justice!
She gave the key for the gate
Should I ever need to lock up
Or feel like keeping people out

(He stops singing.)

GINNY: Well that was okay I guess!
LOT: Think you can do something like that?
    Just sing your thoughts. Just sing your thoughts as they
come to you.
GINNY: I can't.
LOT: I think you can.
GINNY: I don't know.

(She starts singing "Come Clean" by Hilary Duff.)

Let's go back, back to the beginning,
Back to when the earth, the sun, the stars all aligned
'Cause perfect, didn't feel so perfect
Trying to fit a square into a circle was no life
I defy . . .
Let the rain fall down and wake my dreams
Let it wash away my sanity
'Cause I wanna feel the thunder, I wanna scream
Let the rain fall down, I'm coming clean
I'm coming clean

LOT: That was incredible.
GINNY: That was Hilary Duff.
LOT: Who?
GINNY: Hilary Duff.
LOT: Who's that?
GINNY: Lizzie McGuire.

LOT: You didn't write that?

GINNY: No.

LOT: Dang.

(*Now:*

The next day. Justice in Lot's house. Holding a bag.)

JUSTICE: Want a burrito? I have an extra.

LOT (*Taking it*): Okay, maybe.

JUSTICE: Eat it, art monk. Do you have that Kropotkin book
I gave you?

LOT: What book?

JUSTICE: Peter Kropotkin. *The Conquest of Bread.* Pyotr. Pyotr
Kropot—

LOT: Oh that. I used that. Tore out the pages and glued them
on my thing.

JUSTICE: What?

LOT: I apologize.

JUSTICE: Lot, that was from the library.

LOT: I apologize.

JUSTICE: I'm the head librarian!

LOT: I apologize.

JUSTICE: Whatever. Let me see what it became.

LOT: No it's not ready! You're not allowed to look back there.

JUSTICE: Whatever. Did you read it at least?

LOT: As I was tearing and gluing it on.

JUSTICE: Did you like it?

LOT: Socialism. Scarcity. Sharing. Bread. Sure. You trying to get
me to believe in community?

JUSTICE: No. I have no agenda.

LOT: Uh-huh.

JUSTICE: What do you have against community?

LOT: I don't have to have all the same opinions as you.

JUSTICE: Didn't say you did! How's it going with Ginny?

LOT: I don't know. Fine.

JUSTICE: You enjoying it?

LOT: Guess so.

JUSTICE: Good. Y'all writing a song?

LOT: How do I know? It's gonna take years. It's gonna take twelve thousand years. You're giving me anxiety. Light's dying. I have things to do.

JUSTICE: Alright alright. Just eat the burrito. Don't make it art, art monk. Eat the burrito, cowboy. Eat it.

(Now:

> *Lot is recording a song on a tape recorder. He's playing a raw melody on a little keyboard.)*

LOT *(Singing)*:

> A great wall of trash appeared 'round the town
> I couldn't get past that big smelly mound
> I was thinkin' how strange
> This great wall of trash
> So I cut the wall down
> With my little eyelash
>
> It took a long time
> It took a long time
> It took a long time
> It took a long time
>
> I packed it all up
> And I brought the trash home
> Trash older than me
> Trash old as the sea
>
> Weirdos don't ask for help
> No one knew it was me

But I shouldn't complain
Now the people are free

(Now:
Ginny and Lot are in Lot's house. New session.)

LOT: Did you listen to that tape I gave you?

GINNY: What tape?

LOT: I gave you a tape. I sent you home with a tape. It has three songs on it.

GINNY: Oh, I'm not sure.

LOT: You didn't listen to them?

GINNY: No.

LOT: Dangit! I made those songs for you. I wrote three songs for you.

GINNY: Oh, I know.

LOT: And you didn't listen to them?

GINNY: Not yet. I will.

LOT: This is proof about how talking to people is stupid.

GINNY: Please don't say "stupid."

LOT: Why not?

GINNY: I don't like it, please.

LOT: Okay. Do you think my songs are weird? Maybe you think the songs are weird.

GINNY: A little.

LOT: Okay.

GINNY: Yeah.

LOT: You don't like the way I make music.

GINNY: Not really.

LOT: Okay.

GINNY: Yeah.

LOT: I was never trained. So maybe that's why.

GINNY: I like music with more music. And stuff like that.

LOT: Music with more music?

GINNY: I like Celine Dion, NSYNC, Selena Gomez—stuff like that.

LOT: Okay.

GINNY: Hilary Duff, Shawn Mendes, Whitney Houston—stuff like that.

LOT: Right. Who are these people? Whitney Houston I know.

GINNY: Yeah, Whitney Houston.

LOT: Whitney Houston I know. My sister loved her.

GINNY: Right.

LOT: But who's Shawn Mendes?

GINNY: He sings like Prince Legolas.

LOT: Who's that?

GINNY: My husband.

LOT: What?

GINNY: Orlando Bloom. I like when music makes me think about God and dance for my mom. And I don't twerk or stuff like that. My friend Angelo twerks like crazy. And stuff like that.

LOT: I get it. You like pop.

GINNY: There ya go.

LOT: Well I'm not the right person to be teaching anyone pop.

GINNY: But I like country.

LOT: You like country?

GINNY: Yes. Shania Twain, and Dixie Chicks, and Carrie Underwood.

LOT: Oh I don't know them.

GINNY: Who's your favorite singer?

LOT: My favorite singer? Yeah. What's his name?

GINNY: I don't know.

LOT: Well, whatever. I liked my grandfather's voice. Last night I had a dream that I wasn't wearing any shoes, and I was in a room with my grandfather.

And other old men.

And other old men, in a circle.

And they started singing.

Low. Low singing. For a long time.

A low sort of dead singing. For a long time.

I think my favorite music is music like that.

GINNY: Well, that's cool.

LOT: Not really. I don't know anyone's names. I like the song about waiting 'round to die.

GINNY: Oh. Weird.

LOT: Do you know that one?

GINNY: I don't like that one.

LOT: Okay.

(Pause.)

GINNY: I have a crush on someone.

LOT: Who is it?

GINNY: Ben Dickson.

LOT: Who's Ben Dickson?

GINNY: A really cute boy.

LOT: Where'd you meet him?

GINNY: At Special Olympics Bowling.

LOT: Okay congratulations. Does he know you like him?

GINNY: Well he's my boyfriend.

LOT: Okay congratulations.

GINNY: Yeah!

(She's unbearably happy, she does a little dance.)

LOT: What's he like?

GINNY: He's very cute. He's good at bowling. He's fourteen.

LOT: He's fourteen?

GINNY: Yes.

LOT: How old are you?

GINNY: I'm thirty-four.

LOT: Ginny.

GINNY: Yeah.

LOT: Ginny.

GINNY: What?

LOT: You can't.

GINNY: I can't what?

LOT: You're not allowed! Don't you *know* that?

GINNY: Not allowed what? He's my boyfriend.

LOT: No he's not.

GINNY: What?

LOT: Oh no. No—Ginny.

(He starts having a panic attack.)

Sorry. Sorry—I'm sorry. It's gonna get hard for me to speak. Just for a moment.
    Sorry sorry sorry sorry.
    Sorry sorry sorry.
    I'm sorry. It's not a big deal.
    Sorry. It's not a big deal.
    Sorry. Not a big deal.
    Sorry. Not a big deal.
    Sorry.

(He gets very quiet. He tries to breathe. This takes a long time. Eventually, Ginny rubs his back. He flinches, moves away.)

GINNY: Tell me you're okay.

LOT: You just have to be careful, Ginny, okay?

GINNY: About what?

LOT: About who you like. You can't let yourself like the wrong people.

GINNY: Okay. Like who?

LOT: Like Ben Dickson. He's too young. He's just a boy. People don't always know how good you are. They can't always tell.

GINNY: I'm a really good person.

LOT: I bet you are.

GINNY: And Ben is too young, but I'm really good, and he's too young for me, and I'm a grown woman.

LOT: Right.

GINNY: And people need to know that I'm a good person.

LOT: They do.

GINNY: Do they think I'm bad?

LOT: No, but they might just get confused.

GINNY: Well, he's not my boyfriend, and I should not have said that. He's just a volunteer and a cute kid. I need to choose my words carefully.

LOT: I understand.

(He tries to calm down from the panic attack.)

They just don't want what you want to be real. The one thing they never want it to be is real.

GINNY: Yeah. Huh?

LOT: It's not allowed to be real for us. They can't deal with it. They can't let it happen.

GINNY: Who?

LOT: Styrofoam people.

Why would I ever want to be styrofoam? Yeah why would I ever want to be styrofoam? Well because styrofoam people are allowed to *want* things. And if you're special you're just supposed to *need* things. Styrofoam people get to spend time with their wanting. Yeah they lie in bed at night, wanting something. And they dream about it. And they wake up the next day and say: I'm gonna try to get that thing that I want. And they go around trying to get that thing. Just because they want it.

And then someone like me comes around. Or someone like you comes around. Complicated people. Layered people. Granite. Basalt. Obsidian people. We're so complicated people don't want to think about it. So they make us more simple. In their brains. They don't think about it, and they call us simple. And everything is about our *needs*. All our little *needs*. Our special needs. Everyone around us becoming burdened by our constant need. And if there's something that we want? Well it's for them to decide if we really *need* it.

(Pause.)

So, what do you—yeah what do you want, Ginny?
GINNY: I don't know.
LOT: Yes you do.
GINNY: I'm fine.
LOT: Tell me what you want.
GINNY: Ice cream.
LOT: I don't have that.
GINNY: We can go get it. It needs to be fat-free and dairy-free.
LOT: I'm not talking about ice cream.
GINNY: I know.
LOT: I'm talking about what you *want*.
GINNY: I know.
LOT: So tell me.
GINNY: Maybe a Sprite.

(Ginny laughs. Lot laughs for the first time—it bursts out of him strangely.)

Fine. I want a new birthday. Because it's too close to Christmas. And a new family.
LOT: Okay!
GINNY: More of a family. I want a family in California. With lots of pop stars and special kids.
LOT: Great. What else do you want?

GINNY: I want a boyfriend to become a husband. And I want to become a mom.

LOT: Right.

GINNY: And have five blonde kids.

LOT: Okay.

GINNY: And six blonde boyfriends.

LOT: At the same time.

GINNY: Yep. But only one husband. With curly brown hair.

(Lot laughs again. Ginny laughs.)

I just want a different life. And a different house. And a new smile.

LOT: No, your smile is fine.

GINNY: Not really. And people will give it to me, because my mom passed away.

LOT: People will give it to you?

GINNY: She left it in her will.

LOT: She left you a new smile in her will?

GINNY: A new life. I think so.

LOT: Oh. What was it like when your mom died?

GINNY: Hey, stop. I don't know.

LOT: Okay.

(Pause.)

GINNY: We were having a birthday party, it was my birthday party, I was thirty-four years old and my mom was ready in the kitchen to give a big speech about me and before I know it Justice says *oh my God, Leanne, Leanne, I need help, somebody call an ambulance, somebody call an ambulance* and I had no idea what was going on. And the little kids were driving me insane being noisy and disrespectful so I actually slapped a child in the face because I was worried about my mom. And the ambulance came and they could not wake her up and I said *Mom, Mom please wake up* and she would not wake up and later I had to say goodbye. But I feel bad for losing my temper because I should not do that.

LOT: Yeah. That's bad.

GINNY: Oh, that's okay. Because she's happy for me, and checking in on me.

LOT: Good.

GINNY: Because I do have a boyfriend. His name is Tim and he's thirty-five years old. He's a prankster. He actually got water in his brain. He calls me way too much. But he touched my bottom when I asked him not to.

LOT: He did what?

GINNY: Yeah.

(She buries her face in her hands.)

LOT: Oh no. Ginny. He shouldn't have done that. Okay? He should not have done that. You asked him not to.

GINNY: People have to understand touch, and ask for permission, and respect boundaries.

LOT: Yes.

GINNY: Touch can cause problems. And when I said that my brother Christopher touched me, he got in trouble. I was trying to understand the lesson about touch. It wasn't his fault or my fault but it made him cry and get upset.

LOT: Your brother touched you?

GINNY: It was my mistake. About choosing words carefully.

LOT: Ginny, you're confusing me.

GINNY: Oh, don't worry. I'm just getting things off my chest. I need to talk everything out.

(Lot stares at the ground. Ginny puts her hand on his back. He jerks away from her.)

I love you.

LOT: What? Stop it. You're confusing me.

GINNY: Oh, that's okay. I love you.

(Lot stands up. He spits.)

LOT: Sorry.

GINNY: Ew.

LOT: Sorry.

(He walks outside. He walks back inside.)

GINNY: Are you okay?

LOT: Shut up for a second. Just shut up.

(Now:
  Justice and Christopher are in Lot's house. Lot is very upset.)

LOT: This was a bad idea. It's hopeless. I'm done.

JUSTICE: Don't say that, Lot.

LOT: I'm the one who's doing it, I'm the one who knows.

JUSTICE: But we're telling you it's not hopeless.

LOT: You don't know that.

JUSTICE: Neither do you.

CHRISTOPHER: Look I just feel bad.

LOT: Leave me alone all of you, I'm done.

CHRISTOPHER: Okay if that's how you feel—

JUSTICE: No, Christopher, stay for a minute, let's—

LOT: I'm done.

CHRISTOPHER: Yeah, oh man, and look I'm sorry that it got—

JUSTICE: You're not done, Lot.

LOT: Why?

JUSTICE: Because I think it's good for you.

LOT: It's not good for me. You can't just say it's good for me and make it true just by saying it.

JUSTICE: Okay I'm sorry, I thought you said it *was*—

LOT: I changed my mind. That's allowed! It's not good for me it's bad for me. It's hurting me.

CHRISTOPHER: Oh man, I'm so sorry . . .

LOT: I told you to leave.

JUSTICE: Christopher, stay. Lot, what's hurting you about it?

LOT: All of it.

JUSTICE: I want you to be more specific.

LOT: I don't want to be more specific.

JUSTICE: Well you need to be—so that I understand and so that Christopher understands.

LOT: It just hurts. Every second of it hurts me. I'm supposed to help her make a song, well why?

    She doesn't want to make a song. I'm supposed to spend all this time with her, well why?

    She doesn't want to spend time with me.

JUSTICE: She does—she told us that she does. You're projecting, you're reading into things—

CHRISTOPHER: She really does, she's been talking about you nonstop at home—

LOT: I'm bad for her.

JUSTICE: Why are you bad for her?

LOT: Just am.

JUSTICE: Christopher, do you think Lot is good for her?

CHRISTOPHER: Yeah I do, in my opinion.

JUSTICE: And I think so too, and Ginny thinks so too. And if you'd let us bring her in here, she could tell you herself.

LOT: No, don't bring her in here.

JUSTICE: Okay, and why is that?

LOT: I don't want to be around her.

JUSTICE: And why is that?

LOT: I just don't.

JUSTICE: You agreed to do this, don't be a quitter.

LOT: Your word, not mine.

JUSTICE: Was there a thing that happened?

LOT: What do you mean?

JUSTICE: Lot, Ginny called me crying and saying that you were upset at her, so I want you to tell me what happened.

LOT: Nothing happened.

JUSTICE: Nothing happened.

LOT: FINE. Know what it is? I don't know what to do with a goddamn thing she says. She tells me people touch her. Says her own brother touched her. What am I supposed to say to that?

CHRISTOPHER: What?

JUSTICE: She—

CHRISTOPHER: She said that?

(Ginny comes in.)

GINNY: What's taking so long?

LOT: Ginny, out.

GINNY: I actually need to use the bathroom—

LOT: GET OUT OF HERE.

GINNY: Excuse me?

LOT: IT WAS SUPPOSED TO MAKE ME FEEL BRAVE. PEOPLE WERE SUPPOSED TO START COMING IN. I DON'T FEEL BRAVE. I FEEL AFRAID. SO GET THE FUCK OUT.

JUSTICE: LOT—STOP IT!

LOT: WHY ARE YOU DOING THIS TO ME JUSTICE?

JUSTICE: WHAT AM I DOING?

CHRISTOPHER: Ginny maybe we should uh—

GINNY: What did I do?

(Ginny has started to pee her pants. She runs to the bathroom.)

Okay now I'm embarrassed.

CHRISTOPHER: Oh man—

JUSTICE: Oh honey—

(Justice goes to help Ginny. Christopher and Lot sit in a long silence. Finally:)

CHRISTOPHER: I can't believe she—

Just so you, uh—I just . . .

I should say that, uh, oh my God . . .

(After a big sigh:) It was when we were in high school. It was a misunderstanding. She was learning about inappropriate touch in school. They kept talking about it. They were teaching them about not touching *here* and *here*.

(He reluctantly demonstrates touch on the chest and touch on the groin.)

And she went to her teacher and said I touched her there and there. I don't know why. Because of hugs? Because hugs can technically touch those places. Or because we slept in the same bed when we were kids. I don't know. That was the worst day of my life. Well, and I'm sorry if that threw you off. She just . . . she's really, she just . . .

(Lot just stares at the ground.)

God. Just, sorry if . . .

(Ginny comes back. She tries to give Lot a hug. He jerks away— it feels scary. Christopher whispers something in Ginny's ear. She looks at him.)

GINNY: Seriously? I give up.

(Christopher and Ginny leave. Justice looks at Lot, who's catatonic.)

JUSTICE: Don't go down into wherever it is you're going.

(Pause.)

Or do, I guess. What do I know.

(Pause.)

Anyhow, you're not alone. And I felt like things were going pretty okay, for a second. So I don't know what happened. But if you want to talk, I'm here.

(Pause.)

You working on something new back there? I saw that new thing.
  Looks like a mountain. Looks like a whole planet.
  You're building a whole Earth in there?
LOT *(Snapping)*: You're not supposed to look back there.
JUSTICE: Hello.
LOT: Anything I make is a one-way street to God. Then God does whatever He wants with it. It's not for you it's not for me it's just for God. And I'm not your project. I'm nobody's project but God. And when I die it'll be God who takes it all up into Him, not those kids, not the lady with the notepad, not the magazines, not the frames, not you and not me. Just God. So don't look back there. And don't think of me, not ever again. Leave.

(Pause. Eventually Justice exhales.)

JUSTICE: Well. So. I'll come by tomorrow.

LOT: No. You're never coming back here.

JUSTICE: Lot. No. That can't be what this is. How is that what this is?

(He's done talking. It takes her a while to move. Eventually, she leaves.

Now:

> *Lot is by the gate at the front of his property.*
> *He swings it shut.*
> *He wraps the chain.*
> *He locks the padlock.)*

END OF PART ONE

Part Two

A sleek and sexy pop music beat. The beat drops. Ginny emerges in a swirl of glory.

GINNY *(Singing and dancing)*:
    Yeah yeah yeah
    Yeah yeah yeah
    Oh oh oh
    Oh yeah

    This is my chance
    Oh yeah yeah yeah
    This is my love song
    Yeah yeah yeah

    This is my
    Oh yeah
    The way you
    This is my
    Yeah yeah yeah

(The lights are suddenly stripped away. Ginny is alone in her den. She looks at her iPad. She screams.)

THE INTERNET STOPPED WORKING. CHRISTOPHER! THE INTERNET STOPPED WORKING. Oh, I hate this.

(Christopher comes on. He goes to the router. He unplugs every cable from the router. He waits. Yawns. He plugs all the wires back in. Waits.)

CHRISTOPHER: Hm.

GINNY: Is it working?

CHRISTOPHER: Not yet.

(She checks her iPad. It's not working.)

GINNY: This is so frustrating.

CHRISTOPHER: Just give me a second.

GINNY: I hate this.

CHRISTOPHER: I know.

GINNY: What do we do?

CHRISTOPHER: I'll call EarthLink.

GINNY: Please fix it. Please.

CHRISTOPHER: Okay I have to go to work, though. What are you gonna do today?

GINNY: I don't know.

CHRISTOPHER: Maybe I'll call Justice.

GINNY: No I'm fine.

CHRISTOPHER: Well you can't just watch movies and drink soda all day.

GINNY: Well I'm FINE with that. I make my own decisions.

CHRISTOPHER: I know.

GINNY: Actually I'm older than you.

CHRISTOPHER: I know.

GINNY: And a lot of people depend on me. Like friends. The whole town. And I want to see them.

CHRISTOPHER: So let me take you to see them. Let's call them.

GINNY: No, forget about it.

CHRISTOPHER: Why not?

GINNY: No one takes me to see them. Mom takes me to see them.

CHRISTOPHER: Well now I have to be the one to take you.

GINNY: But I don't get excited about it anymore. Because Lot didn't like me. And actually, nobody likes me.

CHRISTOPHER: No, Ginny, that was just . . . that was complicated. Lot's just—

GINNY: It's not just Lot. Because no one talks to me every single night. I can't remember my Facebook password.

CHRISTOPHER: I know. I'm sorry. I know. I tried everything. I couldn't remember it. And I can't remember your email password to reset it. But you don't have to be on Facebook to talk to people.

GINNY: Whatever.

(Unseen, Justice comes into the kitchen with groceries.)

CHRISTOPHER: Ginny? I think maybe we should find someone for you to talk to.

GINNY: Like who?

CHRISTOPHER: Like a therapist or someone.

GINNY: No, are you kidding me? You have to think of something different.

CHRISTOPHER: Okay well how do I do that? If you don't help me come up with ideas.

GINNY: I'm older than you.

CHRISTOPHER: Ginny, I know!

GINNY: I'm older than you, I'm the older sister, and I know how to take care of this family.

CHRISTOPHER: I know—

GINNY: So leave me alone. Jerk. Bitch.

CHRISTOPHER: Ginny, I just don't want you to be—

GINNY: Bitch.

(She storms off and slams the door. From behind the door, we hear her screaming. Christopher stands there. Then he turns and sees Justice in the kitchen.)

JUSTICE: Sorry, didn't want to interrupt.

CHRISTOPHER: What am I doing wrong?

JUSTICE: Nothing, honey. Nothing at all. What do you need?

CHRISTOPHER *(Putting his wrists on his hips)*: I don't need anything. I can handle it. I'm sorry to make you do so much.

JUSTICE: You're not making me do a thing. Look at you, wrists on your hips, exactly like your mom. Look—

(She shows him a picture of Leanne on her phone.)

CHRISTOPHER *(Dropping his hands)*: I didn't even notice.

JUSTICE: It's a good thing. Okay I had a thought. Ready?

CHRISTOPHER: Yeah?

JUSTICE: Get away from here. Go see some of your friends. Yeah? Go up to Dallas. I can stay here.

CHRISTOPHER: Really?

JUSTICE: Really.

CHRISTOPHER: Wow. That didn't even occur to me.

JUSTICE: There's a whole world out there.

CHRISTOPHER: I mean my friend did invite me to his ranch. His family has a—but I shouldn't, I don't want to run away.

JUSTICE: Taking some time to yourself isn't running away.

CHRISTOPHER: Okay. Yeah. Thanks. Maybe. But I really do think I can get things feeling good here again. But thanks. But, uh, how are you?

JUSTICE: How am I?

CHRISTOPHER: How are you?

JUSTICE: How am I? How am I?

How am I? How am I?

How am I?

CHRISTOPHER: Yeah what's happening right now? How are you?

(Now:

Justice goes to Lot's gate. It's locked. She looks at it.

Now:

Christopher comes in. Drunk. Ginny on the couch. She's holding pencils and tapping them against a DVD case.)

CHRISTOPHER: You pencil tapping?

GINNY: Yes.

CHRISTOPHER: You haven't done that in so long.

GINNY: Oh well I do love it.

CHRISTOPHER: One Christmas I just got you a box of pencils. Oh do you remember that little movie I made about it for my film elective? I was like sixteen.

GINNY: Oh I forgot.

CHRISTOPHER: It was called "Pencil Tapper." Why'd I do that in black and white? Pretentious.

(After a beat:) Are you still mad at me?

GINNY: No, just frustrated.

CHRISTOPHER: I'm frustrated too. I don't like fighting. I got a little drunk.

GINNY: Oh boy.

(He sits down next to her.)

CHRISTOPHER: I'm sorry I'm really bad at being a caretaker.

GINNY: I'm a caretaker too.

CHRISTOPHER: I know you are.

GINNY: And a caregiver.

CHRISTOPHER: Right. Yeah. I have a headache. I feel awful.

GINNY: It's not good to drink too much beer.

CHRISTOPHER: It was mezcal.

GINNY: Yeah, see?

CHRISTOPHER: Okay. I just want you to know that I love you a lot. You're my full sister.

GINNY: I'm your half-sister.

CHRISTOPHER: I'm saying that you feel like my full sister.

GINNY: No, I'm your older half-sister.

CHRISTOPHER: I know. Never mind.

GINNY: Because we're not exactly the same, actually. We're different.

CHRISTOPHER: Yeah well the part of you that's a part of me is *her*, and that's my favorite part of me.

GINNY: Huh?

CHRISTOPHER: Whatever.

GINNY: Stop pushing me away.

CHRISTOPHER: What?

GINNY: You're pushing me away.

CHRISTOPHER: No I'm not.

GINNY: I didn't do anything wrong.

CHRISTOPHER: I didn't say you did.

GINNY: You always accuse me of things. I'm not lazy or sneaking soda and I'm healthy and fat-free and dairy-free and I'm taking care of my body by myself. So don't accuse me.

CHRISTOPHER: I wasn't accusing you of anything, Ginny!

GINNY: Yes you were. Because I don't need you to tell me what to do. I need you to help me as a brother who knows about me. Not to give me rules. I know the life that I need to have, and nobody is letting me have that.

CHRISTOPHER: Okay, well me neither!

GINNY: Well I know that!

CHRISTOPHER: I have things I want to make. And I want to date someone. I haven't been touched in like a year and a half.

GINNY: Touch is complicated. So you need to be careful with that.

CHRISTOPHER: Yeah, well, Ginny, you know what? I was really hurt when you told Lot that I touched you. That was really, really hard to hear, because you told me that was a misunderstanding—

GINNY: I know it was a misunderstanding, and that's what I said. I said that to him. Okay? So don't be upset because I understand better now. And you learned how to be better too.

CHRISTOPHER: No, I didn't learn anything, because I didn't do anything. It was only confusing. All I learned was that you know *exactly* how to, just, destroy me. And that you make things up.

GINNY: No I don't. It's about choosing words—

CHRISTOPHER: And that it's impossible, it's just impossible and everything I do is wrong. You're so *mean* to me all the time.

GINNY: What?

CHRISTOPHER: You are. You're being mean to me. I'm trying really hard and you're being mean.

(Pause.)

GINNY: Well, I did not intend . . . oh man I hate this. I did not intend to be mean or rude to you. Come here.

(She hugs him.)

I apologize. From the bottom of my heart.

CHRISTOPHER: I apologize too.

GINNY: You've got edge, bro. You've got issues.

CHRISTOPHER: Bro don't even start.

(They sit there.)

GINNY: Because I'm doing my best.
CHRISTOPHER: I know. Me too. Is it okay that I'm going away this weekend?
GINNY: It's fine. But I want to go out of town too.
CHRISTOPHER: Yeah.

(Pause.)

Would you ever want to move to California?
GINNY: Are you serious?
CHRISTOPHER: Yeah. Would you ever wanna act in movies that I made?
GINNY: Are they gonna be good?
CHRISTOPHER: I hope so?
GINNY: Okay. Can I sing? Like *High School Musical*?
CHRISTOPHER: I mean I don't really like musicals.
GINNY: Oh, are you serious. Grow up.
CHRISTOPHER: Hahaha
GINNY: Hahaha
CHRISTOPHER: I want to make movies again I think. And like really try.
GINNY: Are you kidding me right now?
CHRISTOPHER: About what?
GINNY: You're making a movie with me.
CHRISTOPHER: Maybe. One day. But like how the heck are we gonna go to California? We couldn't even write one song here. I was gonna make a music video for you.
GINNY: Well you can, because I do things for myself. And I can make the song.
CHRISTOPHER: You can?
GINNY: Yeah.
CHRISTOPHER: You promise?

GINNY: I'll make the song and then we can get famous and go to California.

(Christopher laughs and then gets really sad.)

CHRISTOPHER: I don't know what I'm so afraid of.

GINNY: It's okay to be scared of the devil.

CHRISTOPHER: I'm not scared of the devil.

GINNY: You should be. When I get afraid, I get sad, or afraid to leave the room, or leave the bed. And it's okay to be scared of the devil at night, or afraid of getting sunburned.

CHRISTOPHER: Sunburned?

GINNY: Just from the sun. Because you're pale, bro. And we can do things for ourselves. In separate houses.

CHRISTOPHER: You don't want to live with me?

GINNY: Not really. I want to live with Zac Efron.

CHRISTOPHER: Okay fine.

GINNY: That's a deal.

(They shake on it. He gets up. Starts puttering around the kitchen. Chugs some Pedialyte. She starts tapping pencils again, rewriting the conversation under her breath.)

(Whispered): "California?"

"Yes, California."

"Are you serious?"

"Yes. I am. If you write that song."

"I see."

(Now:

Christopher gets home. He's a little drunk. Justice is watching TV with Ginny.)

JUSTICE: Hey, there he is. How was it?

GINNY: Hey buddy-o.

CHRISTOPHER: Who's buddy-o?

GINNY: That's you.

JUSTICE: How was your friends?

CHRISTOPHER: They were okay. Yeah. They're not a very good influence on me. I love them.

JUSTICE: And the ranch?

CHRISTOPHER: Really cool actually, yeah. They've got a really good—it's a cool ranch.

GINNY: Okay are we talking about Doritos?

(They laugh. Christopher sits down between them. They watch the movie.)

CHRISTOPHER: Is that Mariah Carey?

JUSTICE: I don't think so.

GINNY: Yes it is.

JUSTICE: Oh.

CHRISTOPHER: Is this a VHS?

GINNY: Yes it is.

CHRISTOPHER: DVD player still not working?

GINNY: No it's not.

(They watch.)

CHRISTOPHER: Is this that movie *Glitter*?

GINNY: Yup.

CHRISTOPHER: Is the Roku not working?

GINNY: The internet is still not working.

CHRISTOPHER: Seriously?

GINNY: Seriously.

CHRISTOPHER: Jeez. I called EarthLink and the bill is definitely paid. So I guess someone has to come look at it.

GINNY: That would be great.

CHRISTOPHER: Everything's breaking. My phone's barely getting service. Our house is a black hole.

(He gets up to get water. Justice follows him to the kitchen. Christopher finds a manuscript on the table.)

What's this?
JUSTICE: Oh that's nothing. Just something I'm writing.
CHRISTOPHER: You're writing something?
JUSTICE: I'm always writing something.
CHRISTOPHER: You are? Is it fiction?
JUSTICE: Not really. It's about anarchism.
CHRISTOPHER: Oh. Are you an anarchist?
JUSTICE: Yes.
CHRISTOPHER: Nuh-uh.
JUSTICE: Yeah-huh.
CHRISTOPHER: Whoa. Cool. What's like, the . . . what's the like . . .

(Justice puts her hand on the manuscript. She sits down.)

JUSTICE: Well it's about anarchism and gifts. About the belief that humans are fundamentally generous, or at least cooperative. That in our hearts, most of us really do want the good. It's about the evils of centralized power, especially in a country as massive as the USA, let alone a state as big as Texas. It's about an unforgiving land. It's about unrealized utopias. It's about how failing is the point. It's about surrender. It's about small groups. It's about community. It's about the right to well-being. It's about family. It's about the dead. It's about ghosts. It's about gentle chaos. It's about contracts of the heart. And the belief that when a part of the self is given away, is surrendered to the needs of a particular time, in a particular place, then community forms.

From the ghosts of the parts of ourselves we've given away. A new particular body. Born of our own ghosts. I don't know. It's about Texas.

CHRISTOPHER: Oh.

JUSTICE: Yeah.

CHRISTOPHER: Justice, we should hang out more. As adults.

JUSTICE: We should.

(Christopher nods and then sits down.)

CHRISTOPHER: Hey, uh, Justice.

JUSTICE: What's up?

CHRISTOPHER: I think I have to go away for a little bit. Again. For like a week. I'm so sorry.

JUSTICE: Oh yeah? Everything okay?

CHRISTOPHER: Yeah everything's okay, yeah, just . . . yeah my dad's dying.

JUSTICE: What?

CHRISTOPHER: I know. Ridiculous.

JUSTICE: Is it the—

CHRISTOPHER: It's the—yeah, the dialysis just isn't—yeah.

JUSTICE: Oh, Christopher. Jesus Christ. I'm so sorry. Does Ginny know?

CHRISTOPHER: Yeah I told her last, uh—and I'll fly her out if . . . yeah.

JUSTICE: Oh my God. So you're going to Boulder?

CHRISTOPHER: No he lives in New Mexico now.

JUSTICE: Since when?

CHRISTOPHER: Like three years.

JUSTICE: That man. I can't keep up.

CHRISTOPHER: Yeah he went there to go be super-Christian, and . . . yeah his super-Christian other son told me it's like one bad day away from hospice and I asked if I should come and he was like "I don't know," but I don't know, I'm reading between the lines and I'm thinking—I'm thinking yeah I should.

JUSTICE: This is too much. This is too much for a person.

CHRISTOPHER: Yeah, but—actually, a lot of interesting things have been happening.

JUSTICE: Like what?

CHRISTOPHER: It's hard to talk about. It's weird.

JUSTICE: Try me.

CHRISTOPHER: Okay. Uh. Like, I found this letter . . .

JUSTICE: You found a letter?

CHRISTOPHER: I found a letter, yeah. I was trying to build a desk. You know, I've been pretty depressed. Like—yeah, this has been just a pretty depressing house to live in.

JUSTICE: Yeah. It's my favorite house ever. But I hear you.

CHRISTOPHER: Just, okay, yeah, you know when you told me to go see my friends it really woke me up. Since then, I've been trying to pull myself out of . . . all this. And really stare it down. Stare my fears down. Or the—I don't know. And I've been trying to meditate or um—pray. And I've been trying to do little exercises. And I was building this desk . . . I ordered a desk from Target.com and I was trying to build it. But I couldn't find a hammer or screwdriver. And I was looking everywhere for a hammer or screwdriver. And I couldn't find them. And I was looking in like a box . . . like a box of things that were important to me, things to remember, you know?

JUSTICE: Yes.

GINNY: I can't hear the movie.

CHRISTOPHER: Oh, sorry, Ginny.

JUSTICE: Sorry, Ginny.

(They talk at a quieter volume.)

Okay, so you found a box of things to remember.

CHRISTOPHER: Yeah I found a box of things to remember. And I was looking through it, and there were all these things. Like weird mementos, and poems from my ex-girlfriend, et cetera. And then I find this envelope.

And it's addressed to me, in my mom's handwriting.

And it's addressed to my old address, in Denton.

And I'm like "what's this letter." I don't remember receiving this letter.

And I open it and I recognize immediately what it is. It's an apology letter *I* wrote, to my parents when I was like fifteen, and they were still together. I started getting obsessed with film that year, and I was watching as many movies as I could . . . I would get all these movies from the library—

JUSTICE: I remember.

CHRISTOPHER: Oh my gosh—yes! You'd—

JUSTICE: I would order the movies we didn't have from the Dallas library—

CHRISTOPHER: Yes! Even the R-rated ones. You were my hero. So I would bike over there and get these movies, and watch them late at night. I was watching everything on the IMDb Top 250. My grades were tanking but I didn't care—I was in love. But I was really close to finishing the IMDb Top 250, but there were a few that weren't available at the library. Like *12 Monkeys* I think and *Once Upon a Time in the West* and this Danish movie *Festen*. And I didn't know what to do, so I stole my dad's credit card and signed up for Netflix, uh, subscription, but just the two-week free trial, because I thought that I could just watch everything in two weeks, like be the first to check the mail everyday and get the DVDs and mail them back and then cancel the subscription and he would never know. And so I did it—and then I canceled it, and I thought I got away with it. But I guess they charged him for something anyway. And he saw it on his statement. And he got really really mad at me. And this was around the same time that Ginny said that thing about me touching her. And my dad had been the one to take me into the school, to talk to them, and I'd sobbed in front of him, in front of everyone, and said it wasn't true. And he believed me. They all did, I think. But then with this Netflix thing, and me lying, it's like it put everything in a new light. And I remember that he was really mad at me, and I remember, as punishment, I was repainting the kitchen walls—I was painting them that yellow that they still are over there—I was stripping the masking tape from the walls—and I remember that I was really obsessed with *label makers* at the time. My dad had a label maker and I would write out funny labels and put them on things. It was a phase I was in. And there was one that was like "I am Superman"—a label I'd made that said "I am Super-man"—everyone thought it was funny because I would put it, like, on the fridge or the toilet—it was an ongoing bit—but like—okay after I had done this bad thing with Netflix, and I was doing my punishment and painting the walls, I took the masking tape from the walls and I rolled it all into a ball—and I put the "I am Superman" label on it and gave it to them—along with that apology letter—and I gave them these two things as like an offering—and that "I am Superman" tape thing sat on his Bookshelf of Special Things forever . . . and when he moved out, he took it with him . . .

JUSTICE: Wow.

CHRISTOPHER: So everything I just told you was like . . . *what I remembered.*

And then I found the letter.

And in the letter, basically, I was reading it, and it was like— And this was just like . . . last week. And I knew that my dad was sick. And that I might have to go see him. And

I've been so afraid of that. Did you know I started going to therapy?

JUSTICE: You did? Christopher, that's big.

CHRISTOPHER: But I thought I was going there to talk about my mom, but it's ended up being so much about my dad. Knowing that he's my only parent left. Knowing that I'd have to see him, probably, soon, and feeling so afraid of that. And like—*why?*

JUSTICE: Right.

CHRISTOPHER: And so that was all the context while I was looking for this hammer. In the box.

And I find the letter. And I'm like . . . Mom sent this to me? When I was in Denton?

Because I don't remember receiving this at all.

Not at all. And it's postmarked and everything. And it's opened.

And it's like—when did she send this? Why don't I remember this?

And I open it and I read it. And it's just immediately like . . . wow. Dropping into a moment.

So much detail. Like my fifteen-year-old self is time-traveling, giving me this gift. You know?

JUSTICE: Yeah.

CHRISTOPHER: Does that make sense?

JUSTICE: It does. What did the letter say?

CHRISTOPHER: Well it's like "Dear Mom and Dad" and then it like launches into this overwritten description of a dream I was having, and then this sort of treatise on the nature of dreams . . . very overwritten and dramatic. But then I'm woken up out of the dream by my dad shouting "GET OUT OF BED." And then I meet him in the hallway and he starts hitting me, just pummeling me with blows. I'm writing these real events to my parents as like, a story. And in the letter I describe being afraid of waking Ginny up, because my dad is hitting me and I'm like slamming into her door.

JUSTICE: Oh my God. And you didn't remember this?

CHRISTOPHER: I had no memory of this. I'd pushed it down. I knew he hit me when I was a little kid, but I didn't know it happened so late. So then . . . I describe, like . . . seeing my mom in her room, just silently making the bed. Seeing her and how she knows this is happening, and this cold look on her face.

And then I describe, like . . . standing in the hallway, shirtless, my face all red from the beating, wearing corduroy pants that have holes in them, because they would get stuck in the bike wheel when I rode my bike to get movies at the library. And then eventually I go back into my room and I'm all sorrowful. And it's only then that the blows start hurting. And I'm like "maybe I'll just never leave my room." And I start writing this letter to my parents.

And it's like a confessional—like everything I've ever done wrong, I list it for them in the letter . . . and I'm like "I'm going to be a good person, I promise." And "I believe in God, I promise."

And thank you for giving me so much shame.

And thank you for being so hard on me.

And thank you for hitting me.

JUSTICE: Oh, Christopher . . .

CHRISTOPHER: Yeah and I'm reading this and I'm like . . . okay well first of all, it makes so much sense that I'm afraid to go see my dad. I'm literally afraid of him. My body is afraid of him.

JUSTICE: Right.

CHRISTOPHER: And second of all, feeling all this gratitude.

JUSTICE: To your mom?

CHRISTOPHER: Oh—

JUSTICE: For sending the letter.

CHRISTOPHER: Oh. Oh. I was gonna—I mean, yes. But no I was gonna say gratitude to my past self, for writing everything down so accurately. *So* accurately—literally giving this gift to my future self.

JUSTICE: I see. Yes.

CHRISTOPHER: The memory came back intact. Right when I needed it most.

JUSTICE: Yes. I see.

CHRISTOPHER: So then I mentioned this letter up in therapy, of course. And she's like "bring that letter to the next session." So I'm like "okay." So that was last Monday, and then I went to the ranch with my friends this weekend, and we got back late this morning, and I went right to Navarro, and then therapy was right after. And then I had to get a drink.

JUSTICE: Right. Okay. What happened? Oh my God.

CHRISTOPHER: Okay I'm just going to tell you, okay: I did shrooms with my friends at the ranch.

JUSTICE: Mushrooms?

CHRISTOPHER: Yeah, please don't judge me . . . it's actually like really safe, and it's such a wonderful drug, it's like the best drug. It's from the earth. It connects you to everything that's alive on the earth.

JUSTICE: Oh Christopher. Trust me, I know.

CHRISTOPHER: Oh. Haha, oh.

JUSTICE: Was it your first time?

CHRISTOPHER: Yeah, it was. It's amazing!

JUSTICE: Yes. Oh that's so good. Good.

CHRISTOPHER: Okay wow so okay I went into the weekend thinking I would tell my friends about this letter. Like, hey guys want to see the most important object in my life? But I didn't, I just never did. I kept it in my backpack. Instead, I drink this mushroom, like, tea?, that my friend made. And eventually I started having this incredible experience, where I was half-myself and half-my-dad. Like, I literally felt like half of my body was his. But like when he was my age. So half of me was this football-playing Christian in the seventies, and half of me was an out-of-shape failed filmmaker today. And it was the wildest thing— I got really adventurous. I had to like run everywhere and touch everything. And I felt really like . . . masculine. And really invested in performing a certain type of masculinity. But then the me-side of myself was really ashamed that I was doing that. Like super embarrassed that I was running around and touching things and being so masculine . . . but then half of me was like "I have to do this."

And it was this insane act of understanding him.

Understanding what it was like to be inside his body. And to care about the things that he cared about. And to not be able to transfer that way of being into his son. It must have driven him crazy. And that just is what it is. And I forgive him. And that feels complicated and good.

JUSTICE: You seem better. You seem brighter.

CHRISTOPHER: I do?

JUSTICE: You do. Aw, I wanna do shrooms.

CHRISTOPHER: Oh my gosh we should totally do them together. Can we?

JUSTICE: Let's do it.

CHRISTOPHER: Let's find a time and do it. Hahaha. That would be crazy. But I'm into it.

JUSTICE: Me too. It's been too long. I've been desperate for a numinous experience. As I approach the second half of the second half of my life.

CHRISTOPHER: Well I think this could be that. Okay so, but . . . sorry okay so I came back today and I was going to therapy. I brought the letter to therapy like she asked. And I was a little early so I went to McDonald's right next door. And I was in McDonald's reading the letter.

And then I was like, oops, time to go to therapy. So I put the letter in my jacket pocket, on the inside, and walked over there.

And then inside the building, the elevator was taking a long time. Like a really long time, like stopping at every floor. And I was like: *that's weird. So long at every floor. What an elevator mystery.* And then it finally came down and a postal worker came out, like a mailwoman . . . And I was like ohhh of course. That's the answer to the riddle. That's why an elevator would stop so long at every floor. Mystery solved.

And then I walked into therapy and I was like "I brought the letter." And she was like "great." And I reach into my jacket pocket and . . . it's gone.

JUSTICE: No!

CHRISTOPHER: It's just gone. And I start freaking out immediately. Like this can't be happening. And she starts freaking out too—and she's like—*go look for it.*

JUSTICE: Oh my God.

CHRISTOPHER: So I retrace my steps and I go back to look for it and it's nowhere to be found.

It's not in McDonald's, it's not in the trash, it's not on the sidewalk on the way over there. It's gone. And I go back to therapy. And I'm like it's gone. And she's like *holy crap.* And I like can't breathe—and I close my eyes tight. And she's like, okay—"just tell me everything you can that was in the letter." And I'm like okay. So I get out my phone and started writing it all out on my Notes app while I'm talking to her. And I try to remember everything I can. But I feel most of it slipping away forever.

(He remembers something else from the letter. He gets out his phone and types something into the Notes app.)

Sorry.

JUSTICE: You remembered something?

CHRISTOPHER: Yeah. Trying not to forget. All the little . . .

(He tries to remember more, but he can't. He sits there, very still.)

Okay.

JUSTICE: And the letter's just gone?

CHRISTOPHER: It's just gone. Yeah. I see three options:

One. It fell out on the street and was taken by the wind or thrown away as garbage, because who could have known how important it was, because a letter is just paper.

Two. Pickpockets—unlikely but possible, I did walk through a small grouping of young men on my way out of McDonald's.

Three. And this is my preference: It was taken by the postal worker, who was actually an angel—because remember the letter appeared to me mysteriously, addressed to me by my mom, who's dead, and who I keep dreaming about— and the letter vanished as mysteriously as it appeared. So I think she sent it down to me via the United States Postal Service. And then I think she took it back up via the same methods.

Mhm.

(Pause.)

JUSTICE: Christopher?

CHRISTOPHER: Yeah?

JUSTICE: Thank you for that gift.

CHRISTOPHER: What gift?

(Ginny walks up to Christopher.)

GINNY: Get your phone, buddy-o.

CHRISTOPHER: What?

GINNY: Your phone.

(Christopher gets out his phone.)

Now film me.

CHRISTOPHER: What is this?

GINNY: Are you filming.

CHRISTOPHER *(Pressing Record)*: Okay, yes.

GINNY *(To the camera)*: Hi, Dad. This is Ginny. And yes, Daddy-o, you heard that right, because I know you always said "call me Dad," and I could not actually do it because I got upset. Because I did actually know that you were not my blood actual father, and that my mom had some issues and complications with her marriage to you. And how you thought Mom and I were always a team against you. But then you accepted me and took me on, as a daughter. And your son Christopher wants to spend some time with you, to help you to not be sick. And he's a good adult man who helps people feel better. You have a good son, so pray to Jesus to be a good dad, okay? I'm done. I love you.

(Christopher stops filming. Ginny touches his nose.)

Boop.

(Now:
    Christopher is gone. Justice is at the kitchen table. Dishes on it. Ginny is cleaning up.)

GINNY: I have an idea, actually.

(Pause.)

I have an idea, Justice.

(No response. Ginny coughs.)

Justice.

(Ginny comes over to Justice, who looks up finally.)

Are you okay?

JUSTICE: Yes. Sorry. Sorry.

GINNY: Giving me a heart attack. I thought you were dead.

JUSTICE: No, no. Sorry, no. Just beside myself. Sitting here beside myself. A ghost of myself from the future maybe, sitting here, old and droopy, telling me to do something I'm afraid to do.

GINNY: Sitting here like a ghost?

JUSTICE: Yeah. Don't be scared.

GINNY: You're scared.

JUSTICE: I am but it's okay. It's okay. Just don't sit there. Just sit here. Sit here with me.

(Ginny sits where Justice points. There are two empty chairs.)

GINNY: Is this where the ghost is sitting?

JUSTICE: No, she's not sitting there.

GINNY: Oh man, I hate this.

JUSTICE: It's okay. It's just me. It's just everything at once. Me sitting here with your mom . . .

GINNY: You and my mom are ghosts at this table? I hate that.

JUSTICE: And there's a dead man too. It's okay.

GINNY: What dead man? I'm terrified. Three ghosts? This is ridiculous.

JUSTICE: No, it's okay. Sorry. Everyone's happy. Everyone's gentle and nice.

(This is a five-person scene. Justice. Ginny. Justice's Ghost. Leanne's Ghost. The Dead Man.)

GINNY: Are you sure?

JUSTICE: Positive.

GINNY: Just coming to help?

JUSTICE: Exactly. Very helpful.

GINNY: Like how my mom tells me not to do things or how to be good. She comes to me in the night, she sits on my bed. We talk. It's okay, it's not scary.

JUSTICE: Really?

GINNY: Sometimes. And it's okay.

(Pause.)

JUSTICE: She was my best friend.

GINNY: Well I know that.

JUSTICE: She was the funniest person I've ever met in my life.

GINNY: Yep. And she was cranky and bossy.

JUSTICE: Sometimes, yep. She would be making so much fun of me right now.

GINNY: And why is that?

JUSTICE: Because I'm thinking about romantic love, and I told her I would never think about it again. I told her, I swore up and down, we were sitting right here and I told her I. DO NOT. BELIEVE. IN ROMANTIC LOVE. She laughed so hard that she broke the chair. But here I am again. Wanting it. You win, Leanne. But what *is* it? I can't be wanting it again, can I? Why would I want it again? It messed me up wholesale last time. It almost killed me. And it wasn't real, anyway, none of it was real, it was all a brutality and a lie. I am really truly struggling to believe that such love is true and real. I know that I love *you*, and Christopher, and my sisters, and so many goddamn people—

GINNY: I don't like that word.

JUSTICE: Sorry. Sorry. But why does this love for Lot feel different?

GINNY: What? Lot?

JUSTICE: I have a crush on him.

GINNY: Are you kidding me right now?

JUSTICE: Nope. I'm a bozo. I've liked him for a long time.

(Ginny gives Justice a big hug.)

GINNY: Okay, I want to be the Best of Honor.

JUSTICE: The Best of Honor? You mean the Maid of Honor.

GINNY: The Best Maid of Honor.

JUSTICE: Well I don't even know if he likes me back.

GINNY: He does.

JUSTICE: But Ginny I mean this is absurd. This is completely ridiculous. To like him. To love him. But it's not going away. It just gets stronger. I miss him. And yet I have become so deeply cynical. Romantic love. I think that it sounds like an excellent idea in theory, but put into practice it seems nearly impossible. It *is* impossible. I know it is. I already know that I'll fall out of love, because ultimately it's just wanting to be loved and not actually wanting to do the hard work of loving. We retreat back into ourselves. So then you say, what about Rilke, what about two solitudes protecting each other. Okay, that sounds nice, but is it even possible? Don't we just end up eating each other, hating each other, feasting on the hate? It seems like just a simple evolutionary habit, a way of keeping from encountering the self in its full horror.

GINNY: I don't like horror.

JUSTICE: Me neither, but being a person is the most horrifying thing in the world.

GINNY: Well, I actually don't know about that.

JUSTICE: Okay. Fair. Just my opinion.

GINNY: To be a person means to be yourself with God.

JUSTICE: Okay. And that's your opinion.

GINNY: Exactly.

JUSTICE: I look at my parents' love, all of its stubbornness, its hanging-on, despite all the infidelity and silence and abuse, yes okay, they had it for fifty years, but it seemed made up of so much triage and so many labyrinths as to make it almost an optical illusion. And it was a beautiful illusion, but wasn't it just *necessity*? Survival? An octopus changing its color. A marvel of duty and imagination, but nothing actual. Nothing actually *there*. A supreme fiction. Then again, when you see somebody who loves somebody else despite all their flaws and foibles and bullcrap, then I don't know if there's anything better in the whole world. I mean that's just a miracle. Then again, how tragic that we're all trained to believe we deserve a miracle.

GINNY: Well you do.

JUSTICE: Well okay. And then the hardest thing: to allow yourself to be loved knowing all those things about oneself.

GINNY: What things?

JUSTICE: All the horror. All the things. There are so many things wrong with me.

GINNY: Not really.

JUSTICE: There are. Disgusting things. Ridiculous things. I'm a perverted old spy. I'm a hypocrite. I'm a candy-ass.

GINNY: Well, that's okay.

JUSTICE: I really don't think it is. Anyhow, it's too late. He never wants to see me again.

GINNY: Yes, he does.

JUSTICE: No, he doesn't.

GINNY: Well, why not? Did you hurt his feelings?

JUSTICE: I guess so.

GINNY: How?

JUSTICE: I don't know, I guess I . . .

(Pause.)

Oh no.

GINNY: Do you know what you did?

JUSTICE: I think so. I think I lied to him.

GINNY: Well. It's not difficult to say you're sorry. You just have to say it out loud.

JUSTICE: Yeah. I'm scared.

GINNY: It's gonna be okay.

JUSTICE: I don't know if it is. Why am I this way?

GINNY: What way?

JUSTICE: Afraid to ask for what I want. It makes me sneaky. I give so much to people, and secretly the whole time I try to bend things to my liking. Which makes the giving dishonest.

GINNY: And what do you want?

JUSTICE: I don't know. A failed utopia.

GINNY: And what is that?

JUSTICE: I don't know. A family.

GINNY: Okay. Look at me, I get it. Look at me. I don't know why I am the way I am. But I want a husband and a family and a boyfriend. And I'm scared to be alone. And I have a lot of feelings for people. Feelings in my heart and in my body.

JUSTICE: Right, I know that's hard for you.

GINNY: Just listen to me.

JUSTICE: Okay.

GINNY: Because I do have a body as a woman.

JUSTICE: I know.

GINNY: And desire as a woman.

JUSTICE: Right.

GINNY: And I do believe that I deserve it.

JUSTICE: Of course you deserve it.

GINNY: It is hard to want touch. And to want true love. And to want babies. But my mom sat me down and told me that I wasn't allowed.

JUSTICE: She did?

GINNY: And that was not okay to me.

JUSTICE: I'm sure she was just doing her best.

GINNY: Yes, she was doing her best. It's nobody's fault. But she can't tell me not to want what I want, do you understand?

JUSTICE: Yes.

GINNY: Because I love when two people are in love. It's my favorite thing. Even if it's scary or you think about dying in his arms. Or not having the love in your heart anymore. Or falling off the cliff.

JUSTICE: Okay.

GINNY: And so you have to be brave and stick up for yourself. And be honest. And you have to be with your special heart.

JUSTICE: Okay.

GINNY: And you have to love with a special heart, okay?

JUSTICE: Yes.

GINNY: So tell him. It's the right thing.

JUSTICE: You're right.

GINNY: And if you do it, God will fill your whole body. And give you a new body.

(Justice gives Ginny a big hug.)

And tell him that I need to finish my song.

JUSTICE: You want to finish your song?

GINNY: I have to.

JUSTICE: I don't know if he'll want to.

GINNY: He has to. Okay? It's important. Where's that thing?

(Ginny finds the tape recorder. She gives it to Justice.)

How does it start?

(Justice points to the Record button.)

JUSTICE: Ginny, don't say anything about me!
GINNY: Don't worry.

(Ginny pushes Record.)

Okay turn around.
JUSTICE *(Turning around)*: Oh okay.
GINNY: Lot, this is for the song. Follow my instructions. You can make the song sort of sad and "waiting around to die" if you want. But it can also be pop, okay? Pop country. And I forgive you. It's nobody's fault. And I miss your heart.

(Long pause. She closes her eyes.)

When I sing to myself, I'm singing just about love.
    When I sing to myself, it's about love and it's about what I want. I don't know.
    When I sing to myself . . . um. When I sing to myself in my room, I don't want anyone to hear so I sing to myself with the door closed.
    Sometimes I forget that I'm capable.
    Sometimes I forget to be an adult.
    And sometimes I forget that my mom passed away.
    And sometimes I remember.
    And that's it. Wow, that was bad.
    (To Justice:) Nobody is ever going to hear this song. Nobody is ever allowed to hear this song.
JUSTICE: Should I stop?
GINNY: No. I want to try again—

(Now:
    Lot's house. Justice walks in.)

JUSTICE: Lot?

(She looks for him.)

Lot?

(She can't find him. She sits down. She waits. A lot of time passes. The light changes.
   Then Lot comes in. He sees her there.)

LOT: How'd you get in here?

JUSTICE: I just came in.

LOT: But the gate was locked.

JUSTICE: I climbed over it, weirdo.

LOT: That's against the law.

JUSTICE: Uh-huh.

LOT: I could get you arrested.

JUSTICE: So call the police.

LOT: I don't have a telephone.

JUSTICE: I know. Where have you been?

LOT: Working.

JUSTICE: Working where?

LOT: The City of Corsicana Regional Landfill.

JUSTICE: You were working at the dump?

LOT: Yes.

JUSTICE: Why?

LOT: I'm employed there.

JUSTICE: You got a job at the dump?

LOT: Yes.

JUSTICE: Why?

LOT: I wanted to.

JUSTICE: But you're opposed to money.

LOT: It's not about the money. I just wanted to work.

JUSTICE: At the dump.

LOT: At the dump yes.

JUSTICE: Oh because you can get your trash there, for your art.

LOT: No I don't take any of it home with me. I'm not making art.

JUSTICE: . . . Lot.

LOT: I want to be alone.

JUSTICE: Lot what happened?

LOT: Did you hear me?

JUSTICE: Have you called that woman? Have you checked in about your pieces selling?

LOT: Asked her to send the pieces back. All of them. And she did. They're in a box on the porch.

JUSTICE: Lot. No. Why?

LOT: I read her books. She talks about living men like they're dead. I don't want people getting rich off my purity, which doesn't exist, or my mystery, which doesn't exist.

JUSTICE: Okay. Okay, I hear you. I just . . . I thought this was what you wanted.

LOT: No, it's what you wanted me to want.

JUSTICE: Is that really what you think?

LOT: Yes it is.

(Pause.)

JUSTICE: . . . Okay. I can see why you thought that.

LOT: You can?

JUSTICE: Yeah. Oh boy. I'm sorry, Lot. You told me all along the way, and I didn't listen. I thought I knew how you felt, better than you did, and . . . I just . . . I really feel like scum.

LOT: Well don't, don't feel like scum.

JUSTICE: But it's how I feel.

LOT: Okay then.

JUSTICE: Yeah, and it wasn't just that. There were things that I wanted from you, and I wasn't honest, I was a liar, and I pushed you in a direction you didn't wanna go.

LOT: You did?

JUSTICE: Yeah.

LOT: But I did want something.

JUSTICE: You did?

LOT: Yeah. I told you I wanted to grieve open, not closed. I told you that.

JUSTICE: Well I took it too far. Patronizing. Manipulative. I'm so sorry.

LOT: No. Stop being weird.

(Pause.)

I should tell you, uh. So. Yeah I found the root of it upon reflection. And upon reflection what happened was Ginny said she "loved" me.

JUSTICE: Oh . . . yeah? And that upset you?

LOT: Guess so.

JUSTICE: I'm sure she meant it as a friend.

LOT: It's just the whole idea. What do I do—say it back? And then what? It messes everything up.

(Pause.)

JUSTICE: Yeah. That must have been confusing to you. With your history.

LOT: What history?

JUSTICE: When you got kicked out of high school.

LOT: What'd you just say? I never, uh—who told you that?

JUSTICE: Sorry, it's just something I know.

LOT: How do you know things?

JUSTICE: I've lived in this town all my life.

LOT: Well, someone must have told you.

JUSTICE: Fine, the warthog, my ex-husband, he remembered you from the police station.

LOT: He was one of them who took me in?

JUSTICE: He was.

LOT: Yeah. Okay. Yeah. The warthog. Yeah. Sure. So?

JUSTICE: So nothing. Sorry.

LOT: I'm not gonna dig up a fossil just for you to understand something you'll never understand.

JUSTICE: I'm not asking you to dig it up. You don't have to talk about it. Just here if you want to. Like when you drove me to that hospital in Fort Worth. I was grateful for that. So I'm here to take you in, if you want to go in. No, not *take you in*, I said that wrong. I meant into the—into the, just into the . . . the, into the, yeah. You don't have to. You don't have to do anything. Jesus, Lot. Every single word is a whole galaxy. And I'm so bad at it. I'll shut up.

(Pause.)

LOT: Yeah well school wasn't right for me anyway. Always getting kicked out the normal classes, getting stuck on an idea that didn't make sense to anyone but me. So I just stopped going. Then I was just around all day, in the old house. My dad was so mad at me. Couldn't keep up with the guys at the construction company. Body like a stick. Sticking around mother all day. A nuisance. Nothing to do. Then they were trying the special class, it was new, it was an experiment. Special needs. And was I one of them? Dad said this is your last chance. And the teacher liked me. Said I taught *her* things. But then after what happened with that girl, she had to kick me out. No choice. But I didn't do anything.

JUSTICE: I believe you.

LOT: I got confused.

JUSTICE: I believe you.

LOT: She couldn't talk or walk. She was in that class with me. She couldn't talk but I understood her. And I thought

I loved her. Said those words to her. She wrote them back
to me. Drew a picture to say it twice. She was an artist. She
wanted to go into the lake with me. She wanted me to carry
her in. We said let's do it naked—we would write about it,
to each other, with pictures. Like a comic book telling our
future. And it wasn't anything. I don't know—and even if
it was something, it's what she wanted. It's what we both
wanted. And we were kids. And we just wanted to do it,
just go in, naked. That's all. And her mother and father
thought it was more. They thought it was something it
wasn't. They couldn't find her after school and then when
they found her, they saw what they saw, and decided I was
something awful. They called me trash. They made that
word go on forever in me. They made me into something
I wasn't. They called the, yeah, warthogs. The warthogs
came and screamed at me. Took me in. Pushed me. Shoved
me. I spent two nights there. And no matter what I said,
no one believed me. And how's that for community. And
I don't want to keep talking about this.

JUSTICE: Okay. Thank you for telling me.

(Pause. Cautiously:) Skinny-dipping is so fun. I'm glad
you did that. I'm glad you loved her. You're a good man.

LOT: I don't care.

(Long pause.)

JUSTICE: Listen, you're very very beautiful. Lot, you're the most
beautiful guy. And I realized something recently. About the
ghost I've been seeing. I don't think it's a dead man. I think
it's a living man. I think it's you.

LOT: That's ridiculous.

JUSTICE: I think you're like some kinda time traveler.

LOT: No you don't.

JUSTICE: Don't tell me what I do or don't think.

LOT: Yes, okay.

JUSTICE: I think you've been building something incredible here. Something you need to be building—something for yourself—and God—something called art, yeah, but also a time machine, something that can stop the linear progression—something that breaks all the rules and brings us back to ourselves and keeps everyone connected to the invisible world.

LOT: Okay. Thank you for the sermonizing.

JUSTICE: What? I wasn't trying to sermonize.

LOT: I hate sermonizing. No word of God but the silent word. Nothing coming down, only going up. Just leave.

JUSTICE: See, why'd you have to switch like that? That hurt my feelings. I'm right here with you, just listening and responding, not trying to bend anything.

LOT: You're confusing me! You were doing it again! You're telling me I'm a ghost with these magic powers but I'm not a ghost, I'm right here and I never agreed to that!

JUSTICE: Okay. Okay. Damnit. You're right. Forget it. I'm sorry.

(Pause.)

Well this is—Jesus, this is as scary as it gets, but I think I gotta say that I love you.

LOT: Don't say that.

JUSTICE: I will say it. I love you.

LOT: Just don't say the word.

JUSTICE: You can't stop me from saying the word.

LOT: It hurts me.

JUSTICE: Okay I like you then. I like you.

LOT: What does that mean?

JUSTICE: It means that I like you. I always have.

LOT: What does that even mean?

JUSTICE: It means that I have crush on you.

(Pause.)

LOT: I don't know what any of that means.

JUSTICE: Well I don't either. I have no idea what it means. Just that I feel you with me all the time. And when I go to sleep I wish I were holding you. That's what that is.

LOT: You can't like me.

JUSTICE: Says who?

LOT: Says everything. You're normal and I'm fucked.

JUSTICE: No you're not.

LOT: Yes I am.

JUSTICE: Well then so am I. Yeah, so am I. I yearn for you, man. How embarrassing. How weird. How do you feel about that?

LOT: I feel fine about it.

JUSTICE: Yeah?

LOT: I guess so. I have no idea what it means. But I know what you said. And I know that I understand—yeah I understand. And I understand and I know what it is and I understand and I feel it too.

JUSTICE: You do?

LOT: Well I just want to tell you that I don't need you.

JUSTICE: Okay.

LOT: Yeah I don't need you. But I do want you.

JUSTICE: Oh. Okay. Really? Well I—haha, wow.

(They sit in silence for a bit and get nervous and then happy. And then nervous.)

LOT: Well now I'm nervous.

JUSTICE: Me too. Is this real?

LOT: Don't ask me.

JUSTICE: Okay. You're weird.

LOT: So are you.

JUSTICE: Can you give me a hug?

(He approaches her slowly and gives her a hug. Then he pulls away.)

LOT: I should most likely be alone now. And figure this out. Might take a long time.

JUSTICE: Okay, sure. I'll leave, yeah. We'll just . . . okay. Okay. Okay. But do we—okay. I mean I'm gonna need—no, not need. Okay. But—oh.

(She gets the tape recorder out of her purse.)

I want you to know that Ginny wrote a song. Well, the lyrics to a song. She spoke them. And she'd like you to write the music to it. If you like. If you like—just let me know. If you listen to it and if you like the wavelength she's on, you know . . . collaborate with her.

LOT: This again.

JUSTICE: Yeah, this again. It's what she wants. I'm just the messenger. Up to you.

(Justice tries to put the cassette tape in Lot's hand. He keeps his fist clenched tight. She puts it on the ground and leaves.

Now:

    Justice and Christopher with Ginny. Justice puts a tape in a boombox. The song plays through the boombox.)

LOT *(Recorded)*: Alright, this is a version of it, I guess. And hi, Ginny. And just give me a little more time, I guess. I guess I love you, like a friend, and I suppose that scared me. Okay. Sorry.

(He starts singing:)

Nobody is ever going to hear this song
Nobody will be allowed to hear this song
Cuz I'm singing it to myself and you can't hear it
When I sing to myself

It's okay that it's messy
When I sing to myself.
I'm singing just about love
When I sing to myself.
Because the tune I wrote is what I want.
When I sing to myself.
When I sing to myself.

Don't want no one to hear me singing with the door
    closed.
When I sing to myself
When I sing to myself
I forget that I'm grown on my own adventure
And sometimes I forget that my mom passed away.
And sometimes I remember.

(Christopher gets out a guitar and starts playing it.)

CHRISTOPHER *(Singing)*:
    She helped me every day—

GINNY: Excuse me, Christopher? You don't play the guitar.
CHRISTOPHER: Oh yeah, I start taking lessons when I'm forty-five.
GINNY: Like time travel? I'm terrified. That's awesome.

CHRISTOPHER *(Singing)*:
    She helped me every day, but then I'd help her
    She still helps me every day, now I can't help her

I bet she messed with our internet to make us wake up
I think she sent me a letter
I think I'll meet her again
Oh we'll all keep meeting each other

GINNY *(Singing)*:

She used to tell me what to do
I'd get mad and storm into my room
We'd stay up late laughing about princes
She drove me around, she loved too many ice creams

Now Christopher, you go:

CHRISTOPHER *(Singing)*:

Oh my dad didn't die
He couldn't find the Superman guy
On his shelf of special things
We looked for it endlessly
But that's okay because we talked about it
Actually no we didn't talk about it
But looking for it felt like talking about it
And half of me is her, half of me is him, half of me is
    me, half of me is you
And sometimes I forget to be an adult.
And sometimes I forget that my mom passed away.
And sometimes I remember.

GINNY: And now:

(Singing):

This is the Mariah Carey part of the song
This is the Whitney Houston part of the song
This is the Carrie Underwood

This is the Shawn Mendes
This is the Dixie Chicks
I am the Dixie Chicks
I am the Dixie Chicks

Justice, you go:

(At some point, Lot has quietly joined them.)

JUSTICE *(Singing)*:
A song is a family.
It escapes to beyond you.
You get something you sure weren't looking for.
You'll become next to nothing
When you walk through the door
To a place where you've never been before:
The land of the dead,
The land of the dead.
They rise up to gut you.
You let them gut you.
They're just ordinary folk, just like you and me.
Worried 'bout bullshit, feeding on mystery.
Then you find a shape.
And that shape becomes you.
And that shape is called a family.
And the shape is a song.
And the song is a failing.
This song is a failing. A family.

LOT *(Singing)*:
Nobody is ever gonna hear this song
Nobody will be allowed to hear this song
Cuz I'm singing it to myself and you can't hear it
When I sing to myself
When I sing to myself

GINNY *(Singing)*:

> And there's only one more thing that I want to say
> I was riding a ghost, a pterodactyl ghost
> Through everyone's homes just to leave them some ice
>   cream
> Safe in their freezer. Fat-free and dairy-free.
> Just like when Oprah gave everyone cars
> But it's me a pterodactyl, and our ice cream
> Legolas is with me, my husband in the story
> From the book and the movie, we save the world.

ALL *(Singing)*:

> Nobody is ever gonna hear this song
> Nobody will be allowed to hear this song
> Cuz I'm singing it to myself and you can't hear it

GINNY *(Singing)*:

> In my house in Corsicana
> In my room in Corsicana
> In my body in Corsicana, Texas

*(They've found themselves in an unforced circle. There's a pause
after the song ends. Ginny looks at Lot.)*

THE END

EVANSTON SALT COSTS CLIMBING

For Rachel

Thank you to Danya. Wow, we did it. How? Love you. Thank you to the thing underneath everything. Thank you Rachel Sachnoff, Quincy Tyler Bernstine, Jeb Kreager, and Ken Leung, for going down into that feeling for us, over and over again. Thank you to Scott Elliott, Ian Morgan, Teresa Gozzo, Cam Camden, Victoria Keesee, and everyone at The New Group. Thank you to the Griffin at the Signature. Thank you Isabella Byrd, Sarafina Bush, Mikaal Sulaiman, Evan Cook, Joshua Yocom, Ann James, Gigi Buffington, Tilly Evans-Krueger, and Matt Saunders. Thank you Rachel April, Stephen Varnado, Sydneii Colter. Thank you Joan Sergay. Thank you Jacob Robinson. Thank you Justin Kirk, Keira Naughton, and Howard Overshown. Thank you Dustin Wills. Thank you Tyler Kieffer, Masha Tsimring, Jean Kim, Nicholas Hussong, Hannah Wichmann, and Seth Bodie. Thank you Thomas Bradshaw, John MacGregor, Olivier Sultan, Eva Dickerman, Elise Kibler, Jesse Armstrong, Kate Dakota Kremer, Rolin Jones, Adam O'Byrne, Una Jackman, Jay Alix, Rebecca Kitt, The White Heron, Robert Egan, Emily James, Shannon Cochran, Casey Stangl, Jess Chayes, Ben Beckley, J. Smith-Cameron, Pete Simpson, Frank Harts, Michael Shannon, Larry Powell, and Ned Eisenberg. Thank you, John Prine! Thank you Lee and Cheryl Sachnoff. And thank you, Yi Huang. You got me through. You seeing this play, seeing what it was, got me through. I love you. So many more people.

(All there ever was was people.) But one particular person more than any. Rachel, thanks for being my best friend. This book is dedicated to you, aslt.

PRODUCTION HISTORY

Evanston Salt Costs Climbing had its world premiere at White Heron Theatre (Lynne Bolton, President and Artistic Director; Michael Kopko, Producing Director and Co-Artistic Director) in Nantucket, Massachusetts, on August 31, 2018, co-presented with New Neighborhood (Rolin Jones, Artistic Director), Una Jackman, and Rebecca Kitt. It was directed by Dustin Wills. The set design was by Jean Kim, the costume design was by Seth Bodie, the lighting design was by Masha Tsmiring, the sound design was by Tyler Kieffer, the projection design was by Nicholas Hussong; the dramaturg was Graydon Gund, the production stage manager was Hannah Wichmann. The cast was:

PETER	Howard W. Overshown
BASIL	Justin Kirk
MAIWORM	Keira Naughton
JANE JR.	Rachel Sachnoff

Evanston Salt Costs Climbing had its New York premiere at Signature Theatre (Paige Evans, Artistic Director; Timothy J. McClimon, Executive Director) on November 16, 2022, presented by The New Group (Scott Elliott, Founding Artistic Director; Adam Bernstein, Executive Director). It was directed by Danya Taymor. The set design was by Matt Saunders, the costume design was by Sarafina Bush, the lighting design was by Isabella Byrd, the choreography was by Tilly Evans-Krueger, the sound design was by Mikaal Sulaiman, with additional sound design by Evan Cook; the voice and text coach was Gigi Buffington, the production stage manager was Rachel Denise April. The cast was:

PETER	Jeb Kreager
BASIL	Ken Leung
MAIWORM	Quincy Tyler Bernstine
JANE JR.	Rachel Sachnoff

Evanston Salt Costs Climbing was developed at the 2017 Ojai Playwrights Conference (Robert Egan, Producing Artistic Director; Mark Seldis, Managing Director); at White Heron Theatre's Next Step Fest; at Superlab, a developmental laboratory co-produced and co-curated by Clubbed Thumb (Maria Striar, Founder and Producing Artistic Director; Michael Bulger, Producing Director) and Playwrights Horizons; and at The New Group.

CHARACTERS

BASIL, male, Greek, salt truck driver, fifties
PETER, male, Evanstonian, salt truck driver, forties
MAIWORM, female, Evanstonian, public works administrator,
    fifties
JANE JR., female, Evanstonian, volunteer, twenties

SETTING

Evanston, Illinois
Three Januarys
2014
2015
2016

NOTE

The Lady in the Purple Hat appears three times.
She wears a wide-brimmed felt purple hat and an old-flowers
dress.
The first time, she's played by the actor playing Jane Jr.
The second time, she's played by the actor playing Maiworm.
The third time, she's played by the actor playing Peter.

Design is people.

—JANE JACOBS

2014

The break room at the Evanston salt dome. Peter and Basil are drinking coffee. Basil is reading from a sheet of paper.

BASIL: "That summer seemed to last forever. The whole family had been cursed since. Now it wasn't so much a legend as real life. The girl stopped running. As she stopped to catch her breath, she looked back. As she searched, her movements were frantic." The end.

PETER: I like it.

BASIL: Thanks.

PETER: Wait, that's how it ends?

BASIL: Yeh.

PETER: I like it.

BASIL: Thanks.

PETER: I like how it takes place in summer.

BASIL: Yeh.

PETER: Wha'd you do last night?

BASIL: I made a big salad but it was gross. Then for a while, you know, for a pretty long time, I stood at my kitchen window and played with my dick.

PETER: Yeah. I feel that. Did I tell you about the hot tub?

BASIL: No.

PETER: The hot tub's too small for anyone to use. I'm gonna get rid of the hot tub. Hot tubs have zero value. It's like selling used toothbrushes. Basil, I want to kill myself.

(Pause.)

BASIL: You want to end your life?

PETER: Yeah.

BASIL: Well, don't.

(Maiworm enters.)

MAIWORM: Listen to this. They wrote an article about us!

(She holds up the newspaper and reads.)

"EVANSTON SALT COSTS CLIMBING. By Bill Agrigento. Relentless winter storms are driving Evanston's salt costs to approximately $500,000, officials reported in a memo. Evanston city staff will ask aldermen on Monday to approve a purchase of rock salt in the amount of $70,128 from Morton Salt. Evanston Public Works Director Jackie Thorstensen and Assistant Director *Jane Maiworm* wrote in the memo—"

PETER: Oh . . . !

BASIL: Ho ho . . . !

PETER: Mentioned by name.

BASIL: Maiworm here in the paper.

PETER: Maiworm over here. Congratulations Maiworm.

MAIWORM: Thanks ah well it's nothing. But what am I gonna say, that it's not nice? It's nice. Usually in these I'm just *an official*, and meanwhile it's *Jackie Thorstensen said*, and *Jackie Thorstensen said.*

BASIL: Right!

MAIWORM: Anyway.

BASIL: Right!

MAIWORM: Anyway. "'Unfortunately, due to an early snowfall in November and an active December,' Thorstensen and Maiworm reported—

BASIL AND PETER: Maiworm over here!

MAIWORM: "'Unfortunately, due to an early snowfall in November and an active December,' Thorstensen and Maiworm reported, staff needed to spend an additional $70,128 'to ensure salt supplies were not depleted going into the heaviest snowfall of the season thus far, on Dec. 31.'"

BASIL: Right. Hoo-hoo!

MAIWORM: "Officials had reported earlier that snow removal costs are climbing. The city spent a total of $411,261 through the first two big storms of the year, on Dec. 31, and last week's blizzard on Jan. 4. $232,418 of that was for overtime (THAT'S YOU!). Miscellaneous costs included overtime (THAT'S YOU!) for tree removals and pothole repairs, which were needed as a result of the frigid temperatures, officials said." Pretty cool, huh fellows?

BASIL: Interesting, for sure. I didn't know the costs were climbing.

PETER: I knew the costs were climbing. I mean it makes sense.

BASIL: I mean it makes sense, but I didn't know they could climb so high. What does that do to everything?

MAIWORM: Well, it's a pressure on everyone. It's a sharper pressure.

BASIL: More work for us.

MAIWORM: More work for us, exactly.

PETER: But that article isn't really about us, no offense. "Over-time" is not my name. They should write a thing about what's it like on the roads, with the salt.

BASIL: What do you mean what it's like?

PETER: Like about what it's like out there when we're salting the roads.

BASIL: No one wants to read that. We drive, we salt. The end. Stories gotta have . . . . . . like, pull.

MAIWORM: I agree.

PETER: Pool?

BASIL: Pull to pull you in.

MAIWORM: Pull you in exactly. This article's a little more admin-istrative which I think is cool.

PETER: I think it's cool when we salt the roads. Sometimes people honk at us. Things fall down. The light's always changing. I think the noises when it hits the road is good. We have funny conversation in the front. It's cold. It's—

MAIWORM: Hahahaha yep. Well. Fun day already! Uh-oh. You guys gotta hit the road in like four minutes.

BASIL AND PETER: Alright Maiworm.

(Maiworm exits.)

PETER: We get an article written about us and that's what they write. They don't even have our names in it. Fucking Mai-worm gets her name in it. I was just trying to think about how it might be cool to have a thing about Peter and Basil. A story, but instead of written with words, it's written with sounds and ice, that tell the story of Peter and Basil.

BASIL: Get over it. America is upsessed with names. In Greece no one gets names written about. We just live and have meals and do normal human drama. Without worrying about is like: is it fantastic human drama?

PETER: Isn't Greece where all the Drama started?

BASIL: Yeh but now we're so over it.

PETER: Well I'm sorry this isn't Greece.

BASIL: Me too, so. Because. It's warm there.

PETER: Well I'm sorry Evanston is cold.

BASIL: Me too.

(They drink coffee.)

PETER: My daughter's writing a story about me.

BASIL: Oh yeh? What about?

PETER: Just, fuckin . . . about me.

BASIL: Huh. I don't think your daughter's story would have much by way of . . . like, what, pull.

PETER: Fuck you

BASIL: No fuck you haha

PETER: Fuck you

BASIL: No fuck you

PETER: Fuck you haha

BASIL: No fuck you

PETER: Fuck you

BASIL: No fuck you

PETER: Fuck you haha

BASIL: No fuck you

PETER: Fuck you

BASIL: OK hahaha.

PETER: I'm gonna kill you motherfucker I'm gonna fuck you up.

BASIL: No you won't I'm too pretty.

PETER: Pretty how.

BASIL: Just pretty.

PETER: Pretty in what way.

BASIL: Just a pretty guy.

PETER: Hahahaha.

BASIL: Hahaha.

PETER: FUCK laughing. I can't even look my wife in the eyes. The sight of my daughter depresses me. I know she's not gonna be very smart and it just seems like she's gonna become one of those chubby women who work at like a library or a church. That's just how it seems to me. Like a 99% prophecy. And it makes me wanna kill myself.

BASIL: Come on. Stop. Rude.

PETER: Rude to who?

BASIL: To those women.

PETER: It's not rude. Fuck you. Those women are fine. She can be one of them. It's fine. It just makes me wanna kill myself.

BASIL: Yeh. Okay. Peter.

PETER: Never mind. Fuck me. Sorry.

BASIL: Okay no. Mmmmmmmm okay listen. Okay. Let me just try to. Okay. You're reminding me so much of. Never mind. Mmm. Hm. Yeh. No I mean. Right right right.

PETER: Yeah?

BASIL: I mean, it's . . . it's it's it's. Yeh it's definitely hard. Even in Greece. On good days. Pretty days in the sun. Nobody leaves you alone. So you'd just look around and sometimes wanna kinda die. I know. But. At the end of the, whole. It's just. "Come on." Yeh?

PETER: No I mean that makes sense.

BASIL: Yeh, just a little . . . you know, you know who you are. And today's. But today will be better. Hahaha, but. You know we'll have good times in the truck.

PETER: True true true true true.

BASIL: Are you still feeling sadness?

PETER: A little. I can't help it. Are you?

BASIL: No.

PETER: Thanks for trying to cheer me up but it takes a while to sink in. My toes are cold.

BASIL: It's a cold day.

PETER: Negative seventeen. Butta time. Suppa time for us. Butta time.

BASIL: Butta time

PETER: Okay but have you thought about what it would be like to die?

BASIL: Like what, or like what, the feeling?

PETER: The feeling, yeah, of the dying, when it happens, what's going on in your heart or brain.

BASIL: Peter, are you asking me to go down into that feeling with you?

(Maiworm enters.)

MAIWORM: Oh no. I have some bad news and it's bad.

PETER: Okay.

MAIWORM: Bill Agrigento killed himself this morning.

BASIL: Oh no.

PETER: Who the fuck is Bill Agrigento?

MAIWORM: He's the guy who wrote the article about us.

BASIL: Oh no.

PETER: "Evanston Salt Costs Climbing"?

MAIWORM: Yeah.

BASIL: Shit. Sad. Ah!

MAIWORM: We were the last thing he ever wrote about.

(They let this sink in.)

PETER: Is that why he did it?

MAIWORM: I have no possible idea, I don't know. Oh my God. I knew him. He was nice. He loved tea. He lived on Lee Street. He had a whole wall of different tea. He showed me a picture.

(Maiworm exits.)

PETER: Goddamnit.

BASIL: What?

PETER: I wanted to kill myself and then Bill Agrigento did. There's nothing new that can be done.

BASIL: You thought killing yourself was a new thing that could be done?

PETER: I dunno, yeah.

BASIL: That is one of the oldest things to be done, I think, as a human activity.

PETER: Well so there's nothing new that can be done.

BASIL: There are new things that can be done.

PETER: Like what.

BASIL: I dunno. No one has ever done for example uh. This:

(Basil goes up to Peter. He grabs Peter's butt cheeks. He kneels down and talks into Peter's butt.)

Winter bunkfuck, all gas zebra, float off bumbleboy. Float away bumbleboy to a warmer sheeeeeeeen! Happen forever happen ever grip!

(Peter laughs and moves away. He gets really sad.)

PETER: Fuck.

BASIL: What?

PETER: It just . . . it won't go away.

BASIL: Yeh. Fuck. Uh well. Yeh.

(Maiworm enters.)

MAIWORM: I just, hey guys. I just. I've been feeling really rattled by this news, and I just wanted to say: I appreciate everything that you are in my life. You always have a home, in me. And if you ever need anything, please talk to me. You're good men. And.

BASIL AND PETER: Thanks Maiworm.

(Maiworm nods a lot. Then she takes a deep breath. We hear the sound of a salt truck backing into the warehouse. She looks at her watch.)

MAIWORM: Oh, you should probably hit the road. And I should head over to the office. This *day*. This—

(She leaves.)

PETER: We should get on the road.
BASIL: Yeh.

(They get ready to leave.)

Peter, it's pretty simple, you need to be a little more okay with—
PETER: Shut the fuck up, honestly, Basil. You've been patronizing as fuck to me all morning. Ah. Sorry.
BASIL: That's uh
PETER: Uh. I love your story, though. About summer. Really. You should do something with that.

(They head out. Basil leaves first. As he exits, Peter slaps his own face, hard, over and over.

Now:
    Maiworm is standing outside in her nightgown and slippers. Jane Jr. comes outside wrapped in a blanket. There is a snowstorm happening.)

JANE JR.: Mom? What are you doing out here? It's freezing!
MAIWORM: Oh I'm sorry Jane Jr., I was having the most horrible dream. Go back to bed.

JANE JR.: What happened in the dream?

MAIWORM: It was—oh gosh, sorry but, to be honest it was about the dead. All the dead. They were rising up in a blurry chorus, and Bill Agrigento was getting fused into them. It was scary.

JANE JR.: The guy who killed himself? Well now I'm gonna have nightmares about that!

MAIWORM: But then it became about heated permeable pavers.

JANE JR.: What are that? Is those.

MAIWORM: Well they're . . . never mind, they're a new technology. I can't get them out of my head.

JANE JR. (*Shuddering from the cold*): What're they for?

MAIWORM: Well don't worry. They're roads that heat themselves. They're de-icing technology. Permeable paving is paving that lets the water, when it rains, fall on top of it and drain right through to the ground, through to the ground below. The surface is both smooth *and* porous. They invented it so that rainwater didn't have to go through the gutter and all the way under the city and all the way off-site for treatment. But *heated* permeable pavers are permeable pavers with heat things under them. So you can imagine what this means.

JANE JR.: I can?

MAIWORM: It means that during ice storms, the ice melts right away, and the water goes right down into the ground, instead of remaining on the surface and refreezing into ice. So it solves like fifty million problems at once. No more plowing except in extreme cases. No more salt. Anyway I've been looking into it, it's a task I gave myself. So you add all this up, and you can imagine what this means.

JANE JR.: I don't know if I can.

MAIWORM: It's objectively better. Sorry to say. They're trying them out over in Rock Island and Davenport. They worked in Nebraska. And we've got some real curious parties. Polly from Northwestern is even interested in test-ing them out on campus. But gosh, Jane Jr., it would be such a big change. It'd put all the truck guys like Peter and Basil out of work. And imagine the construction. And do I trust a road like that? A ground like that? With little secret characters underneath it? Like is this Evanston or is this Disneyton? Heated permeable pavers. I feel as though they're coming. And one day, acting upon the orders of the dead, they'll rise up from the ground and wrap around us until we—anyway. Just a dream. Just a little nervousness. How was your day?

JANE JR.: It was okay. I helped out a lot at the nursing home.

MAIWORM: That's great. Did you sing?

JANE JR.: Yeah I sang.

MAIWORM: What'd you sing?

JANE JR.: "Angel from Montgomery." Dave Matthews Band version.

MAIWORM: Wish I could have heard it.

JANE JR.: It wasn't very good.

MAIWORM: Oh, look, there go Peter and Basil in the salt truck. It must be late or early, wow! Wave!

(They wave to them. A honk in response.)

JANE JR.: We should go inside. It's so cold.

MAIWORM: Yeah. They're calling it a polar vortex.

JANE JR.: A bipolar vortex?

MAIWORM: No, a polar vortex. I hope everyone's safe on the roads tonight. I just worry for this town.

JANE JR.: Okay but don't worry about the heated permeable pavers, Mom. They're not here yet. It's still salt right now for the roads.

MAIWORM: Anyhow.

(She takes a deep breath. The wind roars.)

It's still salt right now for the roads.

(Now:

Peter and Basil are in the salt truck. They're really cold. Peter is driving.)

BASIL: I was thinking about writing another new story.
PETER *(Coughing a little)*: Huh okm. Cool. Okahm. Sorry. Cool.
BASIL: Based on me, on real things of my life.
PETER: Oh yeah. Good good. Right.

(Peter keeps checking the heat.)

Does it feel like anything's coming out?
BASIL: It's coming, it's warming.
PETER: Hm. Hm. Fuck.
BASIL: It's warming, it's coming. Look.
PETER: Fuck. Yeah. Fuck.
BASIL: It is.
PETER: Hm.
BASIL: See.
PETER: Fuck.
BASIL: Feel it.
PETER: Fuck. Hm. I don't know. Fuck.
BASIL: See.
PETER: Okam
BASIL: Feel it.
PETER: Okam.
BASIL: Feel it. It's okay.
PETER: Yeah? No. Fuck.

(Basil realizes there's no heat coming out.)

BASIL: Fuck.

PETER: Yeah.

BASIL: Fuck. Ah, fuck.

PETER: Yeah, see?

BASIL: Fuck. Fuck.

PETER: Yeah, fuck.

BASIL: I just fuck.

PETER: Yeah I don't think it is.

BASIL: Fuck. But it will.

PETER: I don't think it is.

BASIL: It will, it will, it always does.

PETER: I don't think it will. I don't think IT IS, BASIL.

BASIL: It will. Shh, it's fine, it is.

PETER: I don't know if IT IS, BASIL.

BASIL: Fuck.

PETER: Right?

BASIL: Fuck.

PETER: Right. Right.

BASIL: It might not.

PETER: Right.

BASIL: Fuck.

PETER: It broke. It fucking broke.

BASIL: But why would it break

PETER: The core could be

BASIL: What, clogged

PETER: The tubes could be

BASIL: Leaking?, what

PETER: There's no smell, there's a smell if it's leaking

BASIL: The fan maybe broke

PETER: Or the water froze

BASIL: But there's antifreeze

PETER: Or the antifreeze froze

BASIL: It shouldn't break, it cannot break

PETER: It broke

BASIL: No way, fuck no. The cold has entered my heart.

PETER: The cold has entered my heart. It's minus thirty.

BASIL: Thirty below. Hahaha.

PETER: "Feels like."

BASIL: "Feels like."

PETER: Feels like thirty fucking below.

BASIL: Hahaha "feels like," fuck

PETER: Hahahaha.

BASIL *(Hyper-articulated)*: Hahahahaha, ha ha! Ha! Oh fuck, and an uh and an uh and a haha.

PETER *(Hyper-articulated)*: Yes fuckin ha and a Ha and a Ha and a Bunkfuck.

BASIL: Hahahaha

PETER: Hahahaha FUCK laughing.

BASIL: FUCK laughing.

PETER: Hahahaha.

BASIL: Good.

PETER: Real good.

BASIL: Great stuff.

PETER: Real great stuff. Excellent stuff. Good material.

(He brakes suddenly. The sounds of skidding. They both gasp and brace. It's terrifying. Something thuds in the back. They steady.)

Sorry.

BASIL: Ice. Ice is ice.

PETER: Ice is ice.

BASIL: Yeh. Yeh.

PETER: Yeah. Yeah. We gotta check the chute.

BASIL: Yeh?

PETER: Yeah, we gotta check the chute.

BASIL: Yeh?

PETER *(Opening the door)*: Yeah I think we should—fuck, fuck— ah, fuck, the handle, feel fuck!

BASIL: Fuck.

PETER: Yeah fuck but we gotta check the

BASIL: Chute. Okay. Okay. Fuck. My balls, do you feel that?

PETER: Yeah my balls too.

BASIL: Me balls. Me chattering balls.

PETER: Me and my chattering balls, my chattering balls and me.

BASIL: Haha.

PETER: I ruined it. Dumb.

BASIL: Funny dumb!

PETER: You're too kind sir

BASIL: Sir you're too kind to a mere

PETER: To a mere truck man

BASIL: To a mere

PETER: Sir you're far too kind to a mere

BASIL: Sir you're far too kind

PETER: Ahhh okay let's

BASIL: Yeh let's

PETER: Ooooo okay

BASIL: Okay okay yeh ooooo okay AHHHHH

PETER: AHHHH FUCK AHHH OKAY OKAY OKAY

BASIL: OKAY OKAY

PETER AND BASIL *(Hyper-unison)*: AH OKAY OKAY FUCK FUCK OKAY FUCK HAHA AH FUCK OH OKAY AH

(They burst out of their doors. They fix the chute. They run back—freezing. Peter starts up the truck.)

PETER *(Shivering)*: See that garbage truck?

BASIL *(Shivering)*: What garbage truck?

PETER: Not that truck, that other truck, the one behind us? That truck's been there a year and a half.

BASIL: It's hard to clean those trucks.

PETER: It is, it is hard to clean those trucks. Say things. Say things. Say your story.

BASIL: Say my story
   Ah
   Kay
   Kay
   Ah
   Kay
   Kay
   Ah
   Kay
   Hoo hoo hoo
   My story is
   This thing about how
   Hoo hoo
   OH wait
   is it finally
   is it
PETER: I think
BASIL *(The heat's coming back on)*: I think it's coming on—!
PETER: I think yeah!
BASIL: It is yeh—!
PETER: Yeah
BASIL: Yeh it is!
PETER: It is.
BASIL: Yes. Yeehaw. A yeehaw. And a yes.
PETER: Don't shh don't over-celebrate.
BASIL: Right.
PETER: Don't want to over-celebrate. It hates that.
BASIL: Right. Good. Thanks, truck, for the, thank you.
PETER: Right. Simple thanks. A simple thank you.
BASIL: A simple thank you. Thank you.
PETER: Thank you.
BASIL: Kay
   Kay
   So

My story is still in the storm phase.

Is that okay?

PETER: Sure.

BASIL: Kay. My story's about my yiayia, and about the lady in the purple hat. Believe it or not, I never touched my yiayia.

PETER: What's your yiayia?

BASIL: Yiayia is grandmother.

PETER: Oh okay, I thought it was your dick.

BASIL: No. So I do not touch my yiayia, ever. We never hugged. My yiayia was always sitting far away in rooms. Since the day my parents found me, she doesn't know what to do with me. She doesn't know where I came from. No one does. So she sits far away from me, in all the rooms, when I'm a boy. Kay. But she would tell me stories. My yiayia would tell me a story about this lady, this crying lady in a purple hat. She said that if I ever saw a lady in a purple hat, not to go near this lady. She said this lady would try to take me away. I asked my yiayia why would she take me away? My yiayia didn't know. I asked why was she wearing a purple hat? My yiayia didn't know. *Just don't go near her. Don't let her get too close. She'll take you away.*

And I thought this woman was just a story.

But one day I saw. I saw a lady in a purple hat, at the water. Far away but getting closer. Shouting at me. I ran home, fast.

And I started to see her *everywhere*. No matter where we went. Maybe she was *looking* for me. She walked around, in Thessaloniki. She walked around. And she wore too much makeup.

And she talked to herself. And she just, like, uh, she wore too much makeup. Smeared. You know? And always crying, muttering, far away. But getting closer. And me, always running home.

So that was real life. Kay? So then, forever I'm having this *dream*. This same *dream*. This nightmare. Almost every night.

PETER: Still?

BASIL: Almost every night. Still to this day.

PETER: Damn, so it's some shit you gotta work through.

BASIL: It is, it is some shit I gotta work through. So:

I'm standing in front of my house and there's Yiayia across the street, just my yiayia.

She's crossing slowly, crossing in this old-flowers dress. And I love her.

She gets to the big tree, and she leans against it. Suddenly I realize that she is dying, and I'm scared. I'm a little boy and I'm scared. And behind her the town is burning, or falling into the sea, or freezing up. This part is always different.

But my yiayia is leaning against the tree, and dying, and I can't move. I want to help her but I can't move. I'm afraid to run to help her. I'm afraid to touch her.

I feel the door thick behind me, I feel it there—and I hate that she's dying, she's dying, and she sees me, and she cries to me, and she asks me to come help her.

But I don't.

And I want to yell at her GO AWAY.

But I don't.

And now—ah—she is in front of me.

And she is wearing a purple hat. And she is wearing too much makeup. And her face is not my yiayia's. And I can tell in her eyes, she wants to take me away.

And I am too close to the face, the face of the lady. And then we start to fuse. A sweaty forehead, lipstick teeth uhh-hhh like you know like uhhhhhhhhhh breathing hard, her skin into mine, her bones become mine uhhh like you know what I mean like uhh uhh uhhhhhhhhhhhhhh hahaha and we're in love, we're having sex, laughing, weird, but laughing, hahahaha and also melting like uhhhhhhhhhhhhhh we have the same arms uhhhhh we have the same chest uhhh the same legs uhhhhh the same face, and I am her, I am her, going uhhhhhhhhhhhhhhhh uhhhhhhhhhhhhhhhhhhhhhh-hhhhhhhhhhhhhhhhhhhh

My spine breaks into a million pieces.

And then.

I'm on the ground. I feel an incredible heat, from inside me. I am the heat. Okay, and I see that it *was* my yiayia, that I am my yiayia, and I am dying, and I am on the ground, and I am looking at the little boy who's me, who's also dying, and saying he's sorry, saying *I'm sorry, I'm sorry.*

And the city is burning, or freezing up.

Okay.

Okay. I wake up.

PETER: Okay yeah, you wake up.

BASIL: So I fear that lady in the purple hat.

PETER: So do I, now.

BASIL: Yes.

PETER: Okay.

BASIL: Okay.

PETER: Yeah.

BASIL: But, I don't know. I don't know how to make this into a story. Dreams are kind of boring.

(Pause.)

Some snow.

PETER: Yeah. Boy, eh? Damn.

(The wind roars.)

Fucker. Fuck. Haha. Whatever. Fuck. People are weird. I'm weird. You're weird, Basil.

BASIL: I'm weird? I'm not weird.

PETER: Fuck you. Ridiculous. I don't think I've had a cool dream like that in like fifteen years. When I sleep it's just dark noise pushing hard against my brain and teeth.

BASIL: Are you still feeling sadness?

PETER: Of course. It's fucking everywhere.

BASIL: Why do you look for it everywhere? You are looking for it and so you are finding it.

PETER: Okay then. I fucking hate myself.

BASIL: What—Peter—

PETER: Ah, fuck it. Funny times up here in the,

(He wipes his nose.)

in the truck.

(Now:
    Maiworm's bed. Basil is going down on Maiworm. That happens for a while and it's nice. Then it's done. They sit up, a little too formally.)

MAIWORM: Thanks for going down on me, Basil.

BASIL: No problem, Maiworm.
    (Pause. Referring to the cunnilingus:) Yeh it's funny I love that. Doing that.

MAIWORM: Amazing. Such amazing quality of yours.

BASIL: Haha. Yeh. But. Anyway.

MAIWORM: What was I going to say, earlier?

BASIL: I don't know.

MAIWORM: Darn, what was it.

(They're facing away from each other. Both staring off into space. Basil turns back to her.)

BASIL: It's very nice, Maiworm, that you visit us in the mornings, even though your offices moved farther away.

MAIWORM: It's on the way.

BASIL: It's nice of you. How's your heart?

MAIWORM: My heart?

BASIL: Yeh.

MAIWORM: Physically?

BASIL: No. I like you so much.

(Maiworm turns away.)

MAIWORM: Um, oh, I remember what I was gonna say.

BASIL: Oh yeh?

MAIWORM: Oh yeah so you know how every mid-March I do a cruise? I save a little to do a cruise with Jane Jr.

BASIL: Oh yeh? Okay, I'm in.

MAIWORM: How did you know I was going to ask?

BASIL: I knew, I knew.

MAIWORM: But I haven't even told you where I want to go this year.

BASIL: Where?

MAIWORM: I want to do a Mediterranean cruise.

(Pause.)

Because I want to get to know Greece. From which you are. I like you so much too. What do you think about that?

BASIL: I don't want to do that, okay?

MAIWORM: Oh.

BASIL: You will have fun, though.

MAIWORM: Maybe it was a bad idea, anyway. Because we work together. Maybe that makes it a bad idea.

BASIL: Thessaloniki is not on the Mediterranean. It's on the Aegean.

MAIWORM: Oh, shoot. Well I think the boat scoops up into the Aegean. I think "Mediterranean" is just the headline.

BASIL: I don't want to behold my fuckup fuckoff past from a boat. Okay?

MAIWORM: Oh. Okay.

BASIL: Okay, that's great.

MAIWORM: Okay. Well.

(Pause.)

I was also thinking about doing that Caribbean cruise again that I liked so much.

BASIL: Oh! Great. I'll easily do that with you and Jane Jr., yes!

MAIWORM: Okay, great. That's great. I was so worried there for a second. My brain was like a baked potato.

BASIL: Don't worry. Listen. I had a secret I was meaning to tell you.

MAIWORM: Uh-oh, okay. About your f-up f-off past?

BASIL: Oh. No. Never mind.

MAIWORM: No. What is it?

BASIL: Nothing. Peter is so sad.

MAIWORM: Uh-oh. Really?

BASIL: I worry about him, and maybe we both should.

MAIWORM: How sad? More than usual?

BASIL: He's so curious about death. He's not with me, anymore, when he's with me.

(They hear Jane Jr. out in the kitchen.)

Uh-oh, I'll sneak out. I'll see you at the warehouse?

MAIWORM: Yes, I'll check in with him. Thanks for telling me. Don't freeze out there. Good morning.

(Basil kisses Maiworm on the forehead and then leaves. Maiworm starts dressing for work. Jane Jr. enters.)

JANE JR.: Mom. We have to talk about dark energy.

MAIWORM: Okay. Good morning.

JANE JR.: An old scientist at the nursing home told me that we only know about 4% of the energy in the universe. Dark energy is everything else. So that freaks me out but not because of the universe out there, but because of the universe right here. Like if 96% of everything is unknown, does that mean that everything we *know* about is *also* 96% unknown? Like do we only know 4% about toenails? And so why am I so wrapped up in my problems?

MAIWORM: Yeah.

JANE JR.: You know?

MAIWORM: Yeah.

JANE JR.: It's hard because I know exactly what would solve all my problems. I just want to marry a famous singer. And I want to live with the famous singer in a warm place.

MAIWORM: Yeah, you've mentioned this before. Do you think that's an actionable goal?

JANE JR.: I need your support on this.

MAIWORM: Well—what singer do you want to marry?

JANE JR.: This one singer named Guadalupe X maybe. Honestly I have a list.

MAIWORM: Well—I guess before you marry Guadalupe X you have to get to know Guadalupe X, and before you get to know Guadalupe X you have to meet Guadalupe X.

JANE JR.: Right.

MAIWORM: So you could go to their concerts, right? When they come through to Chicago or Milwaukee. Try to meet them after.

JANE JR.: Incredibly low odds of that.

MAIWORM: So I don't know. Send a message on Twitter or Facebook.

JANE JR.: They get six thousand per day. How do I rise from the dreck? Can we think for a second about how one rises from the dreck?

MAIWORM: Okay, let's think.

(They sit there and think.)

Hey. It's getting late. I should go to the office. Someone from Davenport's coming to talk about heated permeable pavers. Remember my little dream?

JANE JR.: Can we solve one problem at a time, please?

MAIWORM: No, I have to go.

JANE JR.: Okay fine.

MAIWORM: Are you going to the nursing home today?

JANE JR.: No.

MAIWORM: Why not?

JANE JR.: It's too insane out there. Five minutes out there and your cheek skin gets frostbite.

MAIWORM: Yeah but I think you should *do* something today.

JANE JR.: I have something to do tomorrow, but I don't have anything to do today.

MAIWORM: What do you have to do tomorrow?

JANE JR.: Teach myself a dance.

MAIWORM: What dance?

JANE JR.: This dance by Guadalupe X.

MAIWORM: What's it for?

JANE JR.: Just for myself to know.

MAIWORM: Why don't you do it today?

JANE JR.: Because today's not the day I do it. Today's just a day. And I have to get through it.

JANE JR. AND MAIWORM: That rhymed.

MAIWORM: I have an idea.

(Maiworm hands Jane Jr. a book.)

JANE JR.: *The Death and Life of Great American Cities.* By Jane Jacobs.

MAIWORM: It's so good. It's by Jane Jacobs.

JANE JR.: This isn't my thing at all.

MAIWORM: It's my whole thing. She's very readable. She's iconic. She was an amazing woman—no college degree, a journalist, a mom, taking on these powerful, greedy men who were trying to put a highway through Greenwich Village. She organized a movement and she beat them! She wanted neighborhoods, eyes on the street, parks, strangeness, community, love, mess. I love her. And it's easy to lose sight of her in Evanston with our thirty-seven subcommittees.

JANE JR.: Is she why Evanston doesn't have a highway going through it?

MAIWORM: I think, yeah! I think this book might have given them the strength to resist that.

JANE JR.: So that's why it takes so long to get to the airport.

MAIWORM: Hahaha, yep. Alright. Stay warm, stay cozy. You can eat the leftovers from Lucky Platter. Stay warm, stay cozy. Be a bean.

JANE JR.: Okay.

(Maiworm heads out.)

Oh fuck. MOM!!!!!!!!!!!!!!!!!!!!!!!

(Maiworm comes back. Jane Jr. falls onto the ground.)

MAIWORM: What happened?

JANE JR.: I just got so scared. I was thinking about how lucky Dad was to die when he did, because all the coasts will flood, and Florida won't exist, and New York won't exist, and an earthquake will hit the Pacific Northwest, so Seattle and Oregon won't exist, and everyone will come to Evanston. Everyone will come to Evanston, Mom, and we'll look out our window and there will be thousands of people, all the time. And they'll all be so weird.

MAIWORM: Oh, dear. Oh, no. My brain went right to the burden on our infrastructure.

JANE JR.: Let's leave Evanston. Let's live in Corpus Christi, Texas.

MAIWORM: Why?

JANE JR.: It's falling into the sea!

MAIWORM: You want to fall into the sea?

JANE JR.: Maybe just to get it over with!

MAIWORM: This is our home.

JANE JR.: But there's something wrong! There's something under everything and it's making us all want to die! It's pushing out from under everything and it's telling us to die and you can't leave me alone with it.

MAIWORM: To die?

(Jane Jr. nods. Maiworm sighs.)

Do you want to come into work with me?

JANE JR.: No.

MAIWORM: Alright then, you'll just have to figure out your day.

JANE JR.: No kidding.

MAIWORM: I'm sorry I don't know what to say about the thing under everything that wants us to die.

JANE JR.: It's fine.

MAIWORM: I don't know what you want me to say, Jane Jr.! You're getting on my nerves!

JANE JR.: I am?

MAIWORM: Yeah.

JANE JR.: Okay.

MAIWORM: Yes and—sorry. I love you. Sorry. See you tonight. We'll—uh. We're gonna find a way forward. We will.

(Maiworm leaves. Jane Jr. picks up the book.)

JANE JR.: *The Death and Life and Life and Life and Life and Life and Life and Life of Mediocre American Towns.* By Jane Jacobs.

(She throws the book. Then! The dark energy reveals itself to Jane Jr. for a moment. She closes her eyes.

Across town, in the break room, Peter sniffles into a cup of coffee, and the dark energy reveals itself to him, too. He drops the coffee. He digs his nails into his forehead.

Basil enters.)

BASIL: Morning!

2015

The break room. Peter and Basil are drinking coffee. Basil is reading from a sheet of paper.

BASIL: "The next day, he got up early and went to work. While laying the stones down and pressing them into the earth, he thought of Reggie's gigantic arms, and planned his escape." The end.

PETER: I like it.

BASIL: Thanks.

PETER: Wait, that's how it ends?

BASIL: Yeh.

PETER: I like it.

BASIL: Thanks.

PETER: I like that one a lot.

BASIL: Yeh. Thanks.

PETER: Wha'd you do last night?

BASIL: My cats had diarrhea all over, both of them. And then the one-eyed one threw up on my feet. Then for a while, you know, for a pretty long time, I stood at my kitchen window and played with my dick.

PETER: Yeah. I feel that. Did I tell you about the garbage disposal?

BASIL: No.

PETER: The garbage disposal's spitting up chunks of— Basil, I want to kill my wife.

(Pause.)

BASIL: You want to murder her?

PETER: Yeah, and then murder myself.

BASIL: Oh no, what? Don't.

(Maiworm enters.)

MAIWORM: Listen to this. They wrote an article about us! "CHANGES MAY COME FOR NEXT SNOW SEASON IN EVANSTON. By Arthur Hyde . . ."

BASIL: R.I.P. Bill Agrigento.

MAIWORM: R.I.P. Bill Agrigento.

PETER: Who the fuck is Bill Agrigento?

MAIWORM: "Evanston officials said they hope to make changes to their snow-fighting approach this winter season, including employing graphics to get messages to citizens. Jane Maiworm—"

BASIL: Oh!

PETER: Maiworm over here.

MAIWORM: It's just me, so! No Jackie Thorstensen.

BASIL: OH!

PETER: Congratulations Maiworm.

MAIWORM: ". . . Jane Maiworm, the city's assistant public works director in charge of city snow removal operations, told aldermen that 2014 marked the fourth of the past five winters that Evanston has seen above-average totals. Predictions for next winter 'are more of the same,' she said. Overtime (That's you!!) costs ran $312,350 for this winter compared to $722,722 a year ago, Maiworm said. 'The price of salt was very expensive last year,' she said, adding that it went up $25 per ton, hiking the city's material spending from $456,470 to—"

PETER: Hold on, I gotta take this call. This number keeps calling me nonstop.

(He walks off.)

MAIWORM: Should I keep reading?
BASIL: Sure.
MAIWORM: Maybe he wants to hear it though.
BASIL: Yes, maybe he wants to hear it. How's your neck?
MAIWORM: Oh, it's getting a little better.
BASIL: Good. I'm sorry about how much I cried the other day, with your fingers in my mouth.
MAIWORM: Oh, that's completely fine.
BASIL: I was just so happy.
MAIWORM: Me too.
BASIL: Sometimes I feel guilty about our little happiness.
MAIWORM: Why? It's ours.

(Peter comes back in and looks at them.)

". . . hiking the city's material spending from . . ." oh, let's see, let's see . . . "The city's efforts to reduce salt use by combining calcium chloride with beet juice reduced costs somewhat in 2014, but also led to reduced efficacy, as evidenced by an increase in minor vehicular accidents at the end of last winter season. The city devoted an entire week last November to increasing community awareness around best practices during a major snowfall, which included an interactive tour from inside the new salt dome. Maiworm said another big change officials hope to make 'is communicating better with our public' on snow parking regulations and the snow route parking ban. In that regard, Maiworm said she would like to see the use of more graphics in signage, something that other communities use. She introduced a rendering that highlighted the city's odd-even parking rule in a graphic that featured different colors for 'odd' and 'even.' 'Perhaps this is a better way of communicating with people,' she said, noting that 'our residential plowing efforts work best when people move their cars' in compliance with the rules, allowing crews (THAT'S YOU!) to clean the streets off." The end.

BASIL: Ho ho . . . !

Maiworm here in the paper.

(They look at Peter.)

Congratulations Maiworm.

MAIWORM: Well it keeps me up at night when they're confused about the signs. It does.

BASIL: Right. Do you know what keeps me up at night? What do the little bunnies do in the winter?

MAIWORM: Oh yeah?

BASIL: Yeah, so many bunnies in Evanston, what do the bunnies do in the winter?

PETER: Fuck you.

MAIWORM: What, Peter?

PETER: Okay, okay. I'll just sit and then I'll stand.

(He sits down.)

MAIWORM: Sorry I read that article. Is that why you're mad?

(Peter laughs quietly to himself.)

I thought you might want to hear it.

PETER: Why'd you think that?

MAIWORM: Because, because.

PETER: Because what?

MAIWORM: Because you're my colleagues and friends. Doesn't that seem valid?

PETER: No.

MAIWORM: Oh, I didn't know.

BASIL: It is valid.

PETER: No it's not.

BASIL: Yes it is.

MAIWORM: Yeah?

BASIL: Yeh yeh, don't worry, Maiworm. I get it. I liked it.

MAIWORM: It's just a nice morning, and I wanted to share it with you. That felt valid to me.

PETER: Won't be long for nice. Nice for long. It's bout to fucking vortex again.

MAIWORM: I know.

PETER: So yeah. What the fuck, and fuck you.

BASIL: Hey. Stop it, come on.

PETER: Damnit. Sorry I got so mean at you.

MAIWORM: Oh it's okay, I just, I just walked in here, hoping to just talk.

PETER: Yeah. Sorry. Fuck. Hahahaha.

BASIL: Hahaha.

PETER: They should write a thing about what's it like what's it gonna be like when the supervolcano underneath Wyoming erupts, and everyone had to move to Evanston, and what Evanston is gonna do with all the people when they come.

BASIL: No one wants to read that. That's too big for this paper.

MAIWORM: I agree.

BASIL: Too big too heavy.

MAIWORM: Too big exactly, too heavy. This article's a little more administrative which I think is cool.

PETER: I think the terror in your heart when you think about it all ending is good. Fuck I don't know. Because it's cold. It's—

MAIWORM: Hahahaha yep. Well. Local news is important. Uh-oh. You guys gotta hit the road in like four minutes.

(Maiworm exits.)

PETER: My brain's doing a weird thing. It's not letting me stand up and do what I need to do.

BASIL: What do you need to do?

PETER *(Almost laughing)*: You're not gonna believe this.

BASIL: Believe what?

PETER: My wife was in an accident.

BASIL: What?

PETER: Just, fuckin . . . skidded off the road.

BASIL: When?

PETER *(Almost laughing)*: This morning. Just now. She's in a coma.

(Pause.)

BASIL: Fuck you
PETER: No fuck you
BASIL: Fuck you
PETER: No fuck you
BASIL: Fuck you haha
PETER: No fuck you.

(Pause.)

BASIL: What?
PETER: What?

BASIL: Fuck you

PETER: No fuck you

BASIL: Fuck you haha

PETER: No fuck you.

BASIL: What the fuck is going on?

PETER: I just feel bad because I was hating her real bad, real bad today worse than everything. I just couldn't stand to look at her. Can't stand to hear her voice. She's been such a big disappointment to me. I mean I love her, but I was thinking: *I'm gonna kill you motherfucker I'm gonna fuck you up.* What a bad thing to think to myself. But also, just a dumb thought to myself. Because I was tired. And really, I do like her, a lot. And think about how much I've liked her—so much. I've liked her so much more than I haven't liked her. In terms of time. Just that nice comfort of all that time. Of liking her all that time.

BASIL: Peter—she's in a coma?

PETER: She skidded off the road.

BASIL: And you are frozen.

PETER: Yeah, I am.

BASIL: Peter.

PETER: Hahahaha.

BASIL: Peter, you should go to the hospital, I think.

PETER: What?

BASIL: Go see your wife in the hospital. Right now.

PETER: No I mean that makes sense.

BASIL: I can drive you.

PETER: True true true true true.

BASIL: Let's go.

PETER: No. Thanks for trying to help but it takes a while to sink in. My toes are cold.

BASIL: We have to leave.

PETER: Negative thirteen. Butta time. Suppa time for us. Butta time.

(Maiworm enters.)

MAIWORM: Peter. I just got a phone call from the hospital. From my friend Hannah at the hospital.
PETER: Okay.
MAIWORM: She said you hung up. Um, have you heard the news?
PETER: Yeah. There's something in this room. It's not letting me stand up.

(Basil goes over and helps Peter stand up.)

BASIL: Let's all go over to the hospital.
MAIWORM: Yeah.
BASIL: Let's go Peter, yeh?
PETER: Sure. They should write an article about what it was like.
BASIL: What what was like?
PETER: When you got me to stand up.

(They head out.

Now:

Basil drives the salt truck alone. He's listening to a country song. He turns off the song. In the silence, we dip into a view of his bottomless sadness. We shouldn't have access to this.

A thud. He gets out to check the chute. When he's outside, he sees the Lady in the Purple Hat crossing the road. She's muttering to herself. He stares at her until she's gone.

Now:

Jane Jr. is dancing to a pop song by Guadalupe X. She dances very hard. The dance is sensual. The song sounds like it was created by a deep-sea creature. Jane Jr. messes up and screams.

Maiworm enters. Jane Jr. turns off the stereo.)

JANE JR.: Hi. Okay. Wow, I'm sweating.

MAIWORM: You were dancing.

JANE JR.: Yeah, it's that dance by Guadalupe X. Yeah but it's not finished.

MAIWORM: Amazing though.

JANE JR.: Well it took me a year to get around to it.

MAIWORM: It's great that you dance. It's a great thing about you!

JANE JR.: Thanks.

MAIWORM: You can keep dancing right now.

JANE JR.: No, I'm fine.

MAIWORM: You don't like dancing around me.

JANE JR.: Not really.

MAIWORM: Oh. I wish you did. I wish very much that you did.

JANE JR.: I'm sorry, Mom. How was your day?

MAIWORM: It was fine. It was a day. I hated it.

JANE JR.: I'm sorry.

MAIWORM: Not your fault.

JANE JR.: Right, not my fault. So funny that I do that. "Don't say sorry if it's not your fault."

MAIWORM: It's okay.

JANE JR.: I know.

MAIWORM: Can I tell you about my day? And then I want you to tell me about yours.

JANE JR.: Yes, that's fine.

MAIWORM: That's a plan.

JANE JR.: Let's shake on it.

(They shake on it.)

Good. Good handshake.

MAIWORM: Good handshake. So I went to work today and Jackie slapped me on the back and ohhhh
    Oops
    It's my anxiety, one sec.
    Yeah. Yup. Anyway

(She quietly panics.)

JANE JR.: Mom, Mom, Mom.

(Maiworm manages to breathe.)

MAIWORM: Sorry, it's just . . . Peter's wife died.
JANE JR.: What? How?
MAIWORM: I told you she was in a coma.
JANE JR.: No you didn't! When? I haven't seen you very much.
   What happened?
MAIWORM: I could have sworn I told you. The road was icy and
   she skidded into ongoing traffic. Ongoing? Oncoming.
   Traffic. She was in a coma this whole past week. And she
   slipped away this morning. Their daughter was in the back
   seat and thank God the daughter is alive.
JANE JR.: How old's the daughter?
MAIWORM: Six. And oh my God, it's so horrible, and Peter is
   just . . .
      And I have been feeling this guilt.
JANE JR.: What? It's not your fault.
MAIWORM: But why wasn't that road salted? Or salted enough?
JANE JR.: Mom you're not the salter.
MAIWORM: We're going to go forward with them, the heated,
   the heated permeable
      But we'd have to outsource, we'd have to outsource
   all the

(Panic.)

I was looking for solutions. And of course.
   Heated permeable pavers

(Panic.)

And his wife

And then what, I fire him?

JANE JR.: Mom. Um.

Mom. Um.

Shhh. Um.

You're going to be okay. Everything's okay.

You're home now, you're . . . cozy.

MAIWORM: Okay.

JANE JR.: Tell me you're cozy.

MAIWORM: I am cozy. And I asked her what that would do to the budget . . .

JANE JR.: Who?

MAIWORM: Jackie Thorstensen.

JANE JR.: We don't have to talk about work.

MAIWORM: . . . and she showed me the budget, Jane Jr., and my God, the cost. Oh, God.

Heated

Permeable

Pavers

No one knows how to

Put them

In

We'd have to hire a company.

They'd have all their own people—

All their own

All their own guys.

But there is *so* much good about them. So much *good* about them.

What am I going to tell the boys?

JANE JR.: Tell them everything's gonna be okay. That's it. That's all. Start with that.

MAIWORM: Yeah. Yes. Okay. Yes.

(Maiworm lies down. Panic.)

could be heated by solar power, could be hooked up to a central electric grid—

I mean they ain't kidding, team, it's up to seventy degrees—

bioswales are being—gonna make a ton of difference from a gas perspective—

gonna make a ton of difference from a SALT perspective—

JANE JR.: Mom . . .

MAIWORM: so much to, so—proposals and grants—subsections— is it even financially viable to make all streets heated—and Jane Jacobs wouldn't—or Jane Jacobs would—eyes on the street—messier, she'd want it—messier—I'm a disgrace, all our roads hollowed out and empty—delivery trucks and parking garages—no public sphere—she'd hate me— no—a road can be fixed—what do we do? just let sink-holes—where'd I get my officious little soul—

JANE JR.: Mom!

MAIWORM: And the salt companies? The salt companies? And the labor—! Well in Davenport they've developed a mech-anism to lay brick streets, it's like this big slanted platform and as you back up it just slides the bricks into place, that would also work for a permeable brick, so Evanston could in effect put these streets in themselves through public works employees . . .

maybe so maybe so maybe I'll fight for that—

Sorry, sorry . . . Jane Jr., I'm sorry. I'm here. I'm present.

JANE JR.: It's so frustrating when you bring home your work like that.

MAIWORM: I know.

JANE JR.: I just wish that you weren't the Assistant Director of Public Works. I wish you were the Assistant Director of *Private* Works.

MAIWORM: I wish I were the *Director* of Private Works.

JANE JR.: I'm sorry about Peter's wife.

MAIWORM: I know.

JANE JR.: I love you.

(Pause.)

My day was pretty good.

MAIWORM: Oh God, yes, your day.

JANE JR.: My day was pretty bad. Well, I took the bus to go volunteer at the nursing home yay. And the old scientist was telling me about how *Homo Sapiens* have been destroying the earth from the beginning, that's just what we do, we destroy, even farmers and hunter-gatherers in the Amazon, et cetera. And then I was singing "Angel from Montgomery," John Prine version, for the old scientist and he peed without knowing it and the pee was traveling really slowly towards me.

MAIWORM: The pee was traveling towards you?

JANE JR.: Yes. Really slowly towards me across the floor.

MAIWORM: Is it okay if I laugh?

JANE JR.: No.

MAIWORM: Hahahaha.

JANE JR.: Hahaha. So um, your birthday is coming up huh.

MAIWORM: Oh right. I completely forgot.

JANE JR.: So hey what do you want for your birthday?

MAIWORM: Oh I don't know. You don't have to get me anything.

JANE JR.: I want to.

MAIWORM: Jeez. Chocolate vodka? One of those big bouncy balls that you sit on instead of a chair? Who knows.

JANE JR.: Okay thanks because I just want you to have a good birthday this year because you've been working so hard and you need to know that you are loved and appreciated and stuff like that. And one of my intentions for this year is being a better daughter to you but also a better *friend* to you—

(Maiworm is putting her big coat back on.)

Why are you putting that coat back on?

MAIWORM: Oh I just, I have to run back to the office real quick.

JANE JR.: You do?

MAIWORM: Yes—I just have to run back real quick. I need the database.

JANE JR.: Mom.

MAIWORM: I just, I need the database.

(Now:

Maiworm runs into Peter outside the warehouse.)

PETER: Hey, Maiworm.

MAIWORM: Oh my God, Peter. What are you doing here?

PETER: It's my job. What are you doing here?

MAIWORM: Well I'm just—I had to— Oh Peter. How are you doing?

PETER: Yeah I'm alright. Had a dream last night that I was getting back in the truck. Was climbing up the driver's side but the door never came. I was climbing up forever. It was the tallest truck in the world. I told my daughter. She's writing a story about it. Been a while since I had a cool dream like that.

MAIWORM: Okay. Yes. Oh, Peter.

PETER: Oh, what?

MAIWORM: Alright. Well, listen Peter, I'm so sorry, and if there's anything, anything at all I can—

PETER: There's Basil's car. See ya Maiworm.

MAIWORM: Did you get my stew?

PETER: Yeah. My daughter's a picky eater. We mostly do Domino's. Followed by Oreos. Yeah my belly's jiggling all day with Domino's. Yeah. Fuck. I been to hell and back with Domino's.

(Now:
  The salt truck. Music loud.)

PETER: Good to see you again.

BASIL: Likewise brother.

PETER: Longest week of my life. I had to get back in the truck. Yeah I saw the weather forecast and all her family's been around all the fucking time and I can't stand them so when I saw the weather forecast I just fucking called in and was like: I just have to get back in the truck.

BASIL: Right. Well if you want me to drive or anything.

PETER: No I'm good. Hoo hoo hoo. This is a big one. Ooo, hoo hoo, fuck.

BASIL: Yep, heh heh

PETER: Hoo hoo

BASIL: You been eating?

PETER: Yeah, you?

BASIL: Of course, I love eating. How's um, how's the

(Basil turns the music down.)

How's your daughter?

PETER: She's okay, she's okay. She's, uh. To be perfectly honest, I ordered Domino's like three or four times this week. Me and my daughter are like obsessed with it. The medium pan pizza. It's fucking great. We just sit there and watch the pizza tracker.

BASIL: What's the pizza tracker?

PETER: It's a thing on Dominos.com that shows you when they put it in the oven, and when it's out for delivery. It's like a thermometer going long this way, and it just has this red pulse for the different stages of the pizza. We just sit there and watch that.

BASIL: Uh-huh. And how's the, uh, funeral preparation, is that, do you need—

PETER: You heard about that thing about how Nutella can cause cancer?

BASIL: No.

PETER: Oh everyone's saying Nutella can cause cancer.

BASIL: Oh.

PETER: You haven't heard this? It's in all the tweets. And all the articles about the tweets, know what I mean?

BASIL: No I don't. That's sad. I love Nutella.

PETER: Yeah. It's cuz of the palm oil. Cuz apparently palm oil, when you heat it up, it's cancer. And there's a ton of palm oil in Nutella. But who knew that? They didn't know it caused cancer. How could they know that? It's not anything Ferrero did wrong. Ferrero's the company that makes Nutella. I know that cuz my brother-in-law works there. But now all the stores are all pulling Nutella off all the shelves. Yeah it's crazy when I saw the news, I was like, "my brother-in-law works for Ferrero." He sells Nutella to Walmart. He goes down to Arkansas and sells Nutella directly to the Walmart family. They're scared. My brother-in-law. And his friends at the office. The office in New Jersey. They're just people. They see the news on the internet. They drive to work the next day. They're all like: "Oh no—look at this news story. It's about us." "Fuck. I'm gonna kill myself." "Hey, good morning everyone." "Oh hey Gary." "Did you hear the news?" "Yeah we did Gary. Fuck." "I'm so sorry, Gary." "Me too, Francine." "I'm gonna kill myself." "Yeah, just do it, just kill yourself." "No, don't. We'll get through this somehow." "Yeah. Don't worry." "We're all in this together." "I love you." "Fuck don't say you love me." "Why?" "Cuz it hurts, it hurts to love you, it hurts to love all you people." "Fuck." Fuck. One little tweet and suddenly Nutella means cancer. You start to understand why oil companies and, you know, gun people, plastic people, pharmacy people and whatever, fight back. Why they try to stay on top. Cuz they're just people. And they all want to kill themselves.

BASIL: All of them?

PETER: Yeah.

BASIL: Why do they all want to kill themselves?

PETER: Because the world doesn't need us. Not one little bit. It would be better for the world if we all killed ourselves. The planet would thank us. And we all know it.

(He points out the window.)

See, there's my house. Way too many cars. Way too many people.

BASIL: How are you?

PETER: I truck in the summers, you know that right?

BASIL: Of course I do.

PETER: I'll have to figure out what to do with my daughter this summer. Fuck.

BASIL: Well maybe you can stay here and do the summer work with me.

PETER: Fuck no. Don't you hate the summer work?

BASIL: I do, I do hate the summer work. It is so hot, fixing the hot roads.

PETER: Yeah fuck no. Plus I got my summer friends. You know Jason from Montana? All the guys that do trucking around here, all those guys are from Montana. Those Montana boys, I love em. Especially Jason.

BASIL: Cool.

PETER: "If I can't truck it, fuck it," that's what his business card says.

BASIL: Peter . . .

PETER: Yeah?

BASIL: Tell me. Tell me if you want to talk.

PETER: We're talking.

BASIL: About what happened. Just tell me. And I am here.

PETER: Sure.

(Far away, the Lady in the Purple Hat.)

BASIL: Peter . . .

PETER: Yeah?

BASIL: Do you see that lady?

(The truck skids for a moment. Then steadies.)

PETER: Shit. Sorry. Fuck. You know what? That was the same spot, the stretch where my wife—fuck, hold up, I'm gonna back up.

(The sound of a truck backing up. He pulls a lever.)

I'm gonna —

(He dumps a lot of salt on the road. Too much salt. A white mound. He gets out of the truck and spreads it out on the ground. Takes a while. His boots on that salt.

Now:
    The house. Jane Jr. and Basil.)

JANE JR.: Thanks for checking your email. She's at work, so I thought right now would be a good time.

BASIL: Great time. Just finished my shift. So what's your secret plan?

JANE JR.: Okay I was thinking about throwing my mom a surprise party. For her birthday.

BASIL: That sounds like a good plan.

JANE JR.: Great. I've never thrown a surprise party.

BASIL: I've thrown seven.

JANE JR.: Oh good, oh great. Who should we invite?

BASIL: Well. Peter . . .

> Hank.
> Hannah.
> Hiro.
> HJ.
> JIM!
> Parker.
> Greg.
> Dave and Deb.
> Didi.
> Wally Bobkiewicz.
> Jackie?

JANE JR.: Totally. Wait. Hold on. Maybe we shouldn't do this. It's freaking me out. Too many details.

BASIL: Oh okay.

JANE JR.: Let's small talk. Tell me how you are.

BASIL: I'm okay. Stuff, these days, has been a little rough.

JANE JR.: Well maybe we should push through and do the surprise party anyway. As an optimistic act.

BASIL: Maybe so.

JANE JR.: Maybe um. Maybe it could involve alcohol.

BASIL: That's perfect.

JANE JR.: Doesn't she like that bar?

BASIL: Which one?

JANE JR.: That bar over there somewhere?

BASIL: The Celtic Knot?

JANE JR. (*Making his soft C a hard C*): The Celtic Knot. Yeah.

BASIL: Yes, she loves it. She loves the fiddle players.

JANE JR.: Okay good. Good. Blah. I dunno. Maybe it's not the right year to do this party.

BASIL: Oh.

JANE JR.: Damn. I'm so annoying. Sorry.

BASIL: You're not annoying.

JANE JR.: Change of subject, please.

BASIL: Okay. Why's your name Jane Jr.?

JANE JR.: Because my mom's name is Jane.

BASIL: Who, Maiworm?

JANE JR.: Yeah.

BASIL: But she's not your real mother.

JANE JR.: Yes she is.

BASIL: Oh. I thought. Oh.

JANE JR.: When she showed up, I was five, and her name was Jane too, so I crossed my arms and said "Well then I guess I'm Jane Jr.!" And we lived happily ever after. Change of subject please.

BASIL: How do you like being an American young woman?

JANE JR.: Funny you should ask. I feel absolutely nothing about that.

BASIL: Oh.

JANE JR.: That was a joke, okay. It's a terrible place. And it's gonna get worse. You're lucky you're not from here.

BASIL: But I'm here now. And it's nice to be a small man observing things in the new Rome. In the days before the fall. Hopefully I'll be alive to see the nasty emperors' bacchanals. And then—ah! I will feel the stones crack underneath my feet.

JANE JR.: Oh. Okay cool. Okay cool. So, hey, I've been meaning to ask you . . . who *are* you?

BASIL: Who *am* I?

JANE JR.: Sorry, that was rude.

BASIL: No it wasn't. I, um—

JANE JR.: My mom giggles when your name comes up. And sometimes she sighs. Why didn't you come on that cruise with us last year? At the last minute?

BASIL: Oh. Well. My heart was doing a thing it does sometimes, which is where it violently rejects experiences where I might have to pretend to be happier than I am. And I'm usually a pretty happy guy! So I have to listen to my heart!

JANE JR.: Okay but couldn't you just fake it for one *week*? She was so sad when you didn't come. And sometimes you just have to fake it for the people you care about. Sorry.

BASIL: Don't be sorry. You're probably right.

Oh.

Ah.

JANE JR.: Are you okay? Sorry.

BASIL: Yes, I just touched a little sadness for a second. But I moved through it.

JANE JR.: Why were you sad? Cuz of what I said? Sorry.

BASIL: Don't be sorry. I moved through it. I'm fine.

JANE JR.: That fast? Weird. Look, I'm sorry if I made you sad for a second but it's also okay to be sad for a second.

BASIL: Right.

JANE JR.: Look, I'm completely overwhelmed by having to live the rest of my life. I'm completely bored and terrified every second of every day. And I'm so so so—just—very very very lonely.

BASIL: Oh. Mm. Right right right. You're reminding me so much of. Never mind. Listen, Jane Jr. It's as simple as. Hm. Well think of it this way: We're all just: Have you, uh . . . there's:

JANE JR.: What is that? What are you doing? Are you trying to fix me?

BASIL: I don't know. Sorry. I feel a little confused.

(Weird pause. Shockingly long. Basil smiles. Jane Jr. doesn't. She studies him. Basil gets very uncomfortable. Eventually, Basil giggles.)

Ahm . . .

(He finds the book.)

Oh. *The Death and Life of Great American Cities?*

JANE JR.: Yeah.

BASIL: Your mom asked us to read this, and none of us did. Have you read it?

JANE JR.: Not yet. My mom wants me to.

BASIL: I skimmed it and memorized a quote so that she would think I read it:

"There is a quality even meaner
than outright ugliness or disorder,
and this meaner quality
is the dishonest mask of pretended order,
achieved by ignoring
or suppressing
the real order
that is struggling to exist
and to be served."

(Jane Jr. goes to a dark place. Starts to cry.)

Party? Yes or no?

JANE JR.: It's so much pressure. I feel like this is one of those decisions, where I'll look back, and I'll either say: "I'm so fucking mad at myself for not throwing my mom that party." Or: "I'm so fucking mad at myself for throwing my mom such an embarrassing party where I embarrassed myself and my mom and everyone because it was awkward and poorly planned."

BASIL: What about the option where the party is good?

JANE JR.: Oh, isn't Peter's wife's funeral soon?

BASIL: Yes, it's on Saturday.

JANE JR.: Okay, that settles it. No party. Mom will just have a
    sad birthday this year. Out of respect.

BASIL: Okay great. That's great.

(Pause.)

JANE JR.: I guess we'll never be friends.

BASIL: What? Why not?

JANE JR.: You're afraid to be sad in front of people.

(The door suddenly blows open.)

BASIL: Wow!

2016

The break room. Peter and Basil. Behind them, there's no salt. They're holding their coffee. Peter has a boot on his leg. Basil hands Peter his phone.

PETER: What's this?

BASIL: It's my story. On an online literary journal.

PETER: Wow, cool.

BASIL: It's a micro-fiction story. You can hold it in the palm of your hand. You can read it in under three minutes. You can read it right now.

PETER: Cool, wow. Cool font.

BASIL: Are you reading it?

PETER: No my eyes are all stupid. Can you send me the link?

BASIL *(Taking the phone back)*: Sure.

PETER: Look at the boot on my leg.

BASIL: Yes I saw it. What happened to you?

PETER: I tried to drive into Lake Michigan.

BASIL: Oh no. What. Why?

PETER: I knew it wouldn't work. Cuz of the frozen-ness of the lake. But you know that spot where Lee Street ends? The path just rolls right down into the water. Hit the ice and spun out. Just wanted to feel it for a second.

BASIL: Feel what.

PETER: Like maybe it could happen.

BASIL: What could happen.

PETER: Death could happen.

BASIL: Death could always happen.

PETER: Well maybe it *should* happen.

BASIL: But you've got your daughter.

PETER: Yeah, fuck, Basil! I know I've got my daughter.

BASIL: Oh, Peter.

PETER: Fucked up my tibia. Anyway, I did something. I tried something. No matter what you say, I'm a little proud of myself.

(Pause.)

BASIL: Where's all the salt?

(Maiworm enters with Jane Jr.)

Maiworm, where's all the salt? Oh, hi, Jane Jr.

JANE JR.: Hey.

BASIL: What are you doing here?

JANE JR.: My mom made me come in with her. I was spinning out.

BASIL: Right.

PETER: Hi, Jane Jr.

JANE JR.: Hey. Sorry about your life.

PETER: What?

MAIWORM: So, um. Some big news I wanted to tell you.

BASIL: Oh yeah?

PETER: What's that?

MAIWORM *(It's her anxiety)*: Yeah—oops.
     It's my—one sec.

(Maiworm reveals a piece of paper.)

Okay. Sorry about that. This is, uh, from the Department
of Environmental Services. And, uh. Everything's gonna
be okay.

(She starts to read with the seriousness of a eulogy.)

"Despite its many miraculous uses throughout human history, and due to its unique chemical structure, salt spells
disaster for the soil in which it infiltrates. Through ion
exchange, the Sodium ion lodges within the soil and releases
other ions such as Calcium, Magnesium, and Potassium
into the groundwater, as well as increases metal mobiliza-
tion. This causes depletion in the soil and changes the soil
permeability, causing the soil to become impervious, which
blocks water infiltration, reduces soil stability, and decreases
the soil pH and overall fertility. Salt can have impacts on
soil biota, soil welling and crusting, soil electrical conduc-
tivity, soil osmotic potential, soil dispersion, and structural
stability. Salt kills the grass, shrubs, and foliage along the
roadside. Salt primarily causes dehydration, which leads to
foliage damage but also causes osmotic stress that harms
root growth. Salt can lead to plant death and can also cause
a colonization of salt-tolerant species, such as cattails,
thereby reducing species diversity. Salt severely damages
health of wildlife, including birds and mammals. Birds, the
most sensitive wildlife species to salt, often mistake road
salt crystals for seeds or grit, resulting in toxicosis and . . ."

(She suddenly lets out a loud sob.)

JANE JR.: Keep reading, Mom.

MAIWORM: Okay. ". . . resulting in toxicosis and death. Wildlife such as deer and rabbits are also attracted to the roadway to ingest salt crystals, which leads to higher incidents of vehicular accidents. Particularly high concentrations of Sodium and Chloride can be found in snowmelt, which many animals drink to relieve thirst and potentially can cause salt toxicity including dehydration, confusion, and death." The end. So that's what happens to bunnies in the winter. They eat salt and die confused.

BASIL: Oh.

(Maiworm crumples the paper into a ball.)

MAIWORM: And, you know, it's my own way of telling you—with some science, why . . . ummm.

BASIL: You can tell us.

PETER: What's happening here.

JANE JR.: You can do it, Mom.

MAIWORM: Everything's gonna be okay. Have you two ever heard of heated permeable pavers?

PETER: No.

BASIL: Yes.

MAIWORM: What do you know about them?

BASIL: Expensive.

MAIWORM: Yes. And they're, uh, gonna displace you. They're gonna make your jobs obsolete.

BASIL: What are you saying, Maiworm?

MAIWORM: They wouldn't let me hire you for—

(Peter coughs.)

PETER: This fuckin cough, terrible.

BASIL: Sorry, Maiworm, didn't catch that.

MAIWORM: They're objectively better. Sorry to say. They're safer. They're safer. And I fought for a whole year to get you guys trained to install them, but it just doesn't make sense. We have to bring in a company, hire a company, their team, to do it.

PETER: Maiworm, what are you saying? Are you firing us?

MAIWORM: No. I'm warning you.

PETER: What the fuck?

MAIWORM: Sorry. Everything's gonna be okay. What happened was—I spent all year doing the work that terrified me— which is learning everything about heated permeable pavers. And then I got a grant! From the best—from a major environmental foundation, to make it happen, here in Evanston, one block at a time! And the mayor gave me a little, uh, coin thing. And they fired Jackie who was stuck in her ways, and they made me Director.

JANE JR.: Heck yeah!

BASIL: Ho ho!

MAIWORM: Director of Private Works.

BASIL: Amazing.

MAIWORM: I mean Public Works.

BASIL: Amazing.

MAIWORM: What am I gonna say, it's not nice? It's nice. But boys ... big changes are coming. And in all the fury in my mind, I forgot to order the salt for right now. The salt for this moment, right now. So we don't have any salt. And new salt is on the way. The salt from Skokie. The guys from Skokie are gonna salt our roads today.

BASIL: Oh! The Skokie guys!

MAIWORM: But they use too much beet juice. So expect purplish roads this week.

PETER: So wait, lemme get this straight. Salt trucks have had their day in Evanston?

MAIWORM: It may indeed work out that way. I'm so sorry. I wanted to give you some warning, some time to look for new opportunities . . .

PETER: Oh shit.

BASIL: When is this happening?

MAIWORM: Well, not *today*—

JANE JR.: OW! Sorry. I need to cut my toenails.

2017

PETER: Oh shit.

BASIL: When is this happening?

MAIWORM: Well, not *today*—

2018

PETER: Oh shit.

BASIL: When is this happening?

MAIWORM: Well, not *today*—

2019

PETER: Oh shit.

2020

BASIL: When is this—

2021

MAIWORM: Well, not—

2022

PETER: Oh—

20##

BASIL: When—

2###

MAIWORM: Well—

####

JANE JR.: OW! Sorry. I need to cut my toenails.

2016

PETER: Yeah but are we actually talking about this? I've been working here for almost twenty years.

MAIWORM: I know! I'm sorry! Jesus Christ, I'm so sorry. This came out of love for you, Peter. For you. For your wife. I don't want that to happen again. I want to start a foundation for—

PETER: For what?

MAIWORM: For your wife, for that stretch of road. For road safety. A foundation. Maybe you could work at the foundation.

PETER: A foundation for a stretch of road where one woman died?

MAIWORM: Yes, I really think that could make a difference—

PETER: Not only that, she died because her husband didn't salt the road good enough.

MAIWORM: Peter, no . . .

BASIL: No, Peter.

PETER: Why Evanston, that's my question.

MAIWORM: What?

PETER: Why does Evanston have to be the one?

MAIWORM: Not the only one, and I'll tell you why, because—

PETER: Tell me why—

MAIWORM: Well Peter we're a very green city, we were voted— we have—a duty, a reputation, for sustainability.

PETER: See I wondered if you'd say that. That green shit. I'm not making the world any less green than the next guy. And the green shit is probably gonna kill us too. We're humans, we fuck up and die. So what. And I have a reputation as a salt truck guy. And I like that reputation. It's one of the only things I have that I like. Why can't we let anything just fucking *be*—

(Something shifts in the room.)

This fucking room. Does anyone else feel that?

JANE JR.: Yeah.

PETER: There's something in the fucking room.

JANE JR.: Yeah, there's something underneath everything.

MAIWORM: I feel it.

JANE JR.: You do?

MAIWORM: It's horrible. I probably brought it in!

PETER: You didn't bring it in. That shit's been here.

(Suddenly, Maiworm gasps.)

MAIWORM: What did you just say, Basil?

BASIL: What? I didn't say anything. That was Peter.

MAIWORM: No, you just yelled at me. You just screamed at me to Go Away.

BASIL: I did? No I didn't.

MAIWORM: I'm sorry. I'm so sorry!

(Maiworm runs out of the room.)

BASIL: Did I yell that?

PETER: No.

JANE JR.: No. She left her coat! Mom!

(She runs after Maiworm.)

PETER: Fuck. Fuck. Why'd she come in here just to make us feel dread? FUCK!

BASIL: Ah, yeh.

PETER: Fuck. Fuck. You wanna come over for dinner?

BASIL: Sure. Thank you.

PETER: I gotta clean up then! Fuck! It's okay. My daughter and I, we've been trying to, um. Make a game out of it.

BASIL: Should I come over at six?

PETER: Yeah come over at six and we'll talk this shit out.

BASIL: Okay. I should go see if Maiworm is okay. I didn't tell her to Go Away, did I? I've been sleeping with her for three years.

PETER: I know.

BASIL: Oh!

(Basil starts to leave.)

PETER: Hey why didn't you tell me? It made me sad when you wouldn't talk to me like that.

BASIL: Really?

PETER: Yeah. I never knew what the fuck was going on with you except in your dreams and stories.

BASIL: Really?

PETER: Yeah. You live alone, you diddle your dick, you could die alone and no one would know. And I feel like that's how you prefer it and honestly it makes me sad.

BASIL: Well I got so sad when you started hanging out with the Montana boys more than me. Why did you stop being my only friend?

PETER: The fuck?

BASIL: I don't know.

PETER: I don't know. You make me laugh but you don't make me feel better. And you never asked me how I was doing, when my wife died.

BASIL: Yes I did.

PETER: No you didn't.

BASIL: Yes, I did, all the time.

PETER: Well it felt like you didn't really want to know.

BASIL: It felt that way?

PETER: Yeah, it did.

BASIL: Well that is very strange to me.

PETER: Yeah.

BASIL: You wanted me to go down into the feeling with you? I didn't know if I should. Should I go down into it now? I will go down into it now, for you, Peter, if that's what you want.

PETER: No don't do it *now*.

BASIL: You needed it then and I didn't do it. Maybe I was scared.

PETER: Oh *you* were scared?

BASIL: I'm scared. You are scaring me.

You are finding me out, Peter. I tell everyone I don't feel it, but I feel it.

I wake up every night with my own hands choking me to death.

In the morning I pretend I moved through it.
But I never move through it.
And I'm scared. I feel like a little boy.

PETER: Why?

BASIL: Because I'm—I'm—oh no.

PETER: What?

BASIL: I don't know, I don't know.

PETER: Are you okay?

(Basil finds the door behind him.)

BASIL: Oh, is this happening?

PETER: Why are you looking at me like that?

BASIL: There are new things that can be done.

(Basil leaves.)

PETER: What the fuck, Basil? Fuck. It's fucking hot in here all a sudden.

(Now:
The wind roars. Maiworm is walking through the polar vortex. She pushes against the wind. Jane Jr. runs out and finds her.)

JANE JR.: Mom, what are you doing? You left your coat! How am I gonna get home?

(Maiworm gives her the car key.)

MAIWORM: Here's the car key. You head home. I'll walk to work.

JANE JR.: But it's so cold!

MAIWORM: Jane Jr., is this what you've been living with?

JANE JR.: What?

MAIWORM: Is this what it feels like? I didn't know!

JANE JR.: What?

MAIWORM: I'm a horrible mother!

JANE JR.: What?

MAIWORM: I'm a horrible mother!

JANE JR.: WHAT?

MAIWORM: I'M A HORRIBLE STEPMOTHER!!!

JANE JR.: No you're not! Please don't say that! That makes me feel broken.

MAIWORM: What?

JANE JR.: That makes me feel BROKEN!!

MAIWORM: What?

JANE JR.: I JUST MISS YOU ALL THE TIME. EVEN WHEN I'M WITH YOU.

MAIWORM: I'M SORRY I CAN'T HEAR YOU—THIS WIND! GO HOME.

(Jane Jr. leaves. Maiworm walks.

Now:
Basil alone, walking in the storm. He's on his phone.)

BASIL: Maiworm? Are you okay? Call me back!

(He hangs up. His phone rings.)

Hello?

(Pause.)

Yiayia?

(Now:
Jane Jr. alone with a bottle of chocolate vodka.)

JANE JR. *(On the phone)*: Mom? Wally Bobkiewicz called and said you weren't at the office. Where are you?

(She picks up the bottle.)

I'm day-drinking some of your chocolate vodka. It's kind of bad and kind of good. I've gotta make changes this year. Like you, today, you made that change, and it was hard but you *did* it. And I'm so proud of you. And I don't think you're a bad stepmom. You're my mom. And you're good. You're so good. And I think I'm just kind of a bad person. I'm bad at being a person. And I don't think I'll ever find someone. I don't think I'll ever find someone to battle the thing underneath everything, when it comes for us, you know? The two of us making each other braver, getting to a safe place. That'll never happen. I'm just alone and annoying and getting in the way. So I think for me it's really simple: I don't want to keep living. I want to change from living to not living, and I feel so good about this, Mom, I seriously do. But don't worry, I'll go slowly, and—

(Basil is there. Jane Jr. hangs up.)

Basil! Are you okay?

BASIL: Are you?

JANE JR.: Yes yeah. Do you know where my mom is?

BASIL: I was hoping she was here.

JANE JR.: What do we do?

BASIL: Maybe she is at the Celtic Knot or somewhere warm. I'll check everywhere.

JANE JR. *(Making his soft C a hard C)*: Celtic. Okay, I'll stay here in case she comes here.

BASIL: Okay great. Sounds great. I have to find her before the lady in the purple hat finds me. Bye.

JANE JR.: Wait who's the lady in the purple hat?

BASIL: Who knows. The bridge between up here and down there. I'll make sure your mom gets home safe. Bye.

JANE JR.: You're a hero!

BASIL: No I'm not. You asked me who am I. Who I am is: one day outta nowhere, I left my wife and children in Greece, that's who I am. Bye.

JANE JR.: Wait Basil. Why'd you do that?

BASIL: Why?

JANE JR.: Yeah.

BASIL: Because. Why? Because I . . . no. Fuck. Okay. Fuck. Because I . . . oh God.

(He inhales. He can't say it.)

JANE JR.: You can say it.

BASIL: No I can't. Why? Okay. I left because.

(He looks at her.)

Because they wouldn't fucking leave me alone.

(He looks away from her.)

I don't want to be part of this anymore.

JANE JR.: Wait, Basil. Thank you for telling me. When you walked in here, it got like twenty degrees warmer. Did you feel that?

BASIL: Oh, wow.

(He leaves.)

JANE JR.: It really did, I'm not kidding. Oh, zang, it's so hot. Oh whoa.

(Now:
    Maiworm is sitting at the stretch of road where Peter's wife had her accident. We know it's the spot because there's so much salt there.

The wind and the cold are unbearable. Basil pushes against the vortex and finds Maiworm.)

BASIL: Maiworm, you'll freeze to death!

MAIWORM: Basil?

BASIL: Maiworm, I came to give you my heat. And I don't want you to blame yourself for what is about to happen.

(Suddenly, the Lady in the Purple Hat is behind Basil. She whips Basil around and speaks into his face. Then she whips him back around. Then she's gone.)

MAIWORM: Ma'am? Ma'am?

(Basil's reeling. Dying.)

Who was that? What did she say to you? Basil are you okay?

(Basil hugs Maiworm. He holds her as he falls.)

BASIL: Am I her? Am I you? Are we fusing?

MAIWORM: Fusing?

BASIL: You're freezing up. Take my heat.

MAIWORM: Well I can't take your heat—you need it! Ah, oh God!

BASIL: I need to give it to you!

MAIWORM: Wow, it's so hot. It's burning up! Oh my God!

BASIL: Too hot?

MAIWORM: Not too hot!

BASIL: Uhhhhhhhhhhh

MAIWORM: Ahhhhhhhhhhh

(Basil takes Maiworm down to the ground with him.)

BASIL *(Whispered)*: I'm sorry, I'm sorry

MAIWORM: Basil?

BASIL: I'm sorry, I'm sorry

MAIWORM: For what

BASIL: I'm sorry

MAIWORM: For what? Basil. Don't. Next year you move in with us.

BASIL: And then the next year I move out.

MAIWORM: But we're happy.

BASIL: Sometimes. You were the closest I ever felt to not running away.

MAIWORM: So stay.

BASIL: No.

MAIWORM: I don't understand. When is this happening?

BASIL: Silently one night outta nowhere.

MAIWORM: But why? Basil—no. Not you, Basil. I didn't know.

BASIL: You did know.

(He curls up. The road opens up.)

And you must tell Peter not to follow me down.

MAIWORM: Oh no—Basil—HELP—oh Basil, you're—
    You're just a little boy
    You're just a little boy

*(The wind dies down. Basil's gone. His body goes under the road.
Silence. Maiworm can't understand what's happening.
    Basil comes up Jane Jacobs, who immediately starts mutter-
ing to herself and walking away from Maiworm.)*

BASIL/JANE JACOBS: No, no, no! Horrible. Horrible, every second of it. Tearing up the road here. What is this, salt? Pah, pah.

*(She spits out salt from her mouth. She keeps walking. Maiworm
walks after her.)*

Hole in this road. I hate people who tear up roads. Pah, pah.

MAIWORM: Excuse me ma'am, are you—?

BASIL/JANE JACOBS: Leave me alone.

MAIWORM: YOU'RE—Jane Jacobs?

BASIL/JANE JACOBS: Pah. Pah. Uck.

MAIWORM: Can I ask you—ma'am, I'm a tremendous fan. Can I ask you?

BASIL/JANE JACOBS: What is it?

MAIWORM: I'm trying— We're dying—skidding off—

BASIL/JANE JACOBS: What is the *question*?

MAIWORM: Should I do it? There's this new road de-icing technology. It would go under the roads—it would put people out of jobs, but it would go under the roads—

BASIL/JANE JACOBS: I don't know a damn thing about it. People die. People skid off. The ice melts. The ice conquers. Horrible fucking thing. No one allowed to see each other anymore. No one allowed to regenerate anymore. Why am I seeing this horrible thing? Why am I looking at you? Get away from me.

MAIWORM: Mrs. Jacobs—

BASIL/JANE JACOBS: Don't do anything. Dissolve. Walk around. And wait for it all to end.

MAIWORM: But Evanston needs me.

BASIL/JANE JACOBS: Bland town—already ruined—pah uck this salt—

MAIWORM: Evanston's not so bland. I just want to understand—

BASIL/JANE JACOBS: Stop it! Stop trying to understand! A city is organized *mystery*. If you can *understand* a city then it's already dead. I guess you want everyone dead! This place should be leveled!

MAIWORM: No, no! I don't! Don't say that about Evanston! This isn't like you, Mrs. Jacobs! You're an optimist!

BASIL/JANE JACOBS: No I'm not! You must not have read my later books!

MAIWORM: Oh God—I just want to fix the road!

BASIL/JANE JACOBS: Fine! Do what you want! Layering new sham on top of old sham, mistakes of the living on top of the mistakes of the dead. Fix the road, you pitiful administrator!

MAIWORM: No! Administration is *service*! Every day! That's what I *do*! I just keep chipping away at it—bit by bit—and if I get *specific*—things can be *solved*. Instead of all this—what is *this*—this waiting—just frigging *waiting*? Lie around and wait for the Big Horrible Unknown and then wake up, and there's a wall of water? Wake up, and we can't breathe, we're burning up? Wake up, and my husband's collapsed on the driveway, Bill Agrigento's hanging in the bathroom, my daughter's trapped inside herself, Peter's wife is dead on a road we *promised* her would be safe, and now Basil's, Basil's, where is he, what's happening . . . no! I can't! I'm not just going to wait. I want to wake up and fix some tiny things. A few tiny things. Get up and get to fixing some *specific tininess*, and then some specific tininess after that, and then our little nervousness will become a little happiness. It must, it must do that, while we're here, right? I think I have to believe that. And now that I've felt it, felt what Jane Jr. feels, the thing underneath everything, how big it is—I think I believe in tininess even more now. Get up and get to fixing. Like you did. Doesn't that seem valid?

BASIL/JANE JACOBS: My dear Jane, no. It's too late. I assure you. All of us in the invisible world already know it. Invisible cities sustained by the certainty of your extinction. All you can do is discover people. All there ever was was people. Discover your neighbors. Discover your children. When the sirens blare, you need to know each other, know where to gather, know each other's voices . . .

MAIWORM: Where are you going?

BASIL/JANE JACOBS: Horrible.

MAIWORM: Where's Basil?

BASIL/JANE JACOBS: That little boy? He died laughing under the road.

(Maiworm is alone. In front of her, the road blazes with heat. She weeps. An approaching car honks—

Now:

Jane Jr. is screaming. Peter hobbles into the room.)

PETER: What happened?

JANE JR.: I read a whole fucking book!!! It took me two fucking years!!!

PETER: That's wonderful. What was the book about?

JANE JR.: The death and life of great American cities. And walking around and being STRANGE. I LOVED IT.

PETER: Can you be quieter? My daughter's sleeping in the other room.

JANE JR.: Okay, sorry. She's really cute.

PETER: Okay. I have a confession. I ordered a pizza.

JANE JR.: From where?

PETER: Domino's. They just put it in the oven. See?

(He shows her his phone.)

JANE JR.: Oh cool, the pizza tracker. Do you want to hear me sing?

PETER: Okay, yeah, sing. What are you gonna sing?

JANE JR.: "Angel from Montgomery." Bonnie Raitt version.

PETER: Okay, great.

(Pause.)

Are you gonna sing it.

JANE JR.: Yeah. Can you turn around?
PETER: Sure.

(He turns around.)

JANE JR.: Okay. How'm I gonna do this?

(Singing:)

> I am an old woman,
> Named after—

I can't.
PETER: What?
JANE JR.: I just can't do it.
PETER: Just do it. Sing.
JANE JR.: I just can't.
PETER: Why not?
JANE JR.: I don't know.
PETER: Just do it.
JANE JR.: I can't do it. How?
PETER: Just the fucking doing.
JANE JR.: No.

(Singing:)

> I am an old woman,
> Named after my mother
> My old man is another—

I can't.
PETER: WHAT?
JANE JR.: I can't.
PETER: Yes you can.
JANE JR.: No I can't haha
PETER: Yes you can haha

JANE JR.: No

PETER: Yes

JANE JR.: Fuck you

PETER: No fuck you

JANE JR.: No fuck you

PETER: No fuck YOU

JANE JR.: No fuck you haha

PETER: NO FUCK YOU!
    Fuck you.
    Fuck you. Fucking sing.

(He gets a call.)

One sec.

(He answers. He receives the following gravely.)

Hello? Oh. Really. Oh my God. Okay. Fuck. Is there anything I can do? Fuck, okay.

(He hangs up.)

That was Domino's. They can't deliver the pizza.

JANE JR.: Why not?

PETER: It's too fucking vortexy.

JANE JR. *(Singing beautifully)*:
    I am an old woman
    Named after my mother
    My old man is another
    Child who's grown old
    If dreams were lightning
    And thunder were desire
    This old house would've burned down

A long time ago
Make me an angel
That flies from Montgomery
Make me a poster
Of an old rodeo
Just give me one thing
That I can hold on to
To believe in this livin'
Is just a hard way to go
There's flies in the kitchen
I can hear 'em there buzzin'
And I ain't done nothing
Since I woke up today
How the hell can a person
Go to work in the morning
Then come home in the evening
And have nothing to say?

(Peter claps.)

Thanks.

PETER: How old are you?

JANE JR.: Thirty-one.

PETER: What the fuck?

JANE JR.: What?

PETER: Why'm I babysitting you?

JANE JR.: I don't fucking know!

PETER: Why'd your mom beg me to come here?

JANE JR.: Because do you ever feel like your mom hates being around you?

PETER: Yeah. So?

JANE JR.: Well and because I left her a weird voicemail.

PETER: About what?

JANE JR.: ABOUT SUICIDE, PETER.

PETER: Are you suicidal?

JANE JR.: Maybe.

PETER: I am.

JANE JR.: Really?

PETER: Yeah.

JANE JR.: Why?

PETER: Why are you?

JANE JR.: Because I . . . I don't know because I don't

I can't

I don't

(Her fingers are flapping against her head.)

I want to . . .

(With her arms: "give & give & give.")

But instead I just . . .

(With her arms: "take & take & take.")

PETER: Listen I think, though, that, uh . . . you aren't actually gonna kill yourself silently one night outta nowhere. Maybe you just like looking at the shadow body of it? You want to touch it but not wanna marry it?

JANE JR.: Says who.

PETER: Says me. I read this new micro-fiction story by Basil, I can send you the link. And in it, there's this character based on me. And he talks about suicide, but really what he's talking about is love for the invisible world. Or some shit. I need to read it again.

JANE JR.: Oh, weird. That's—I want to read that.

PETER: I'll send you the link.

JANE JR.: Thanks. Um, do you think there's something underneath everything that wants us to die?

PETER: 100%. I know it to be true.

JANE JR.: Okay cool. Okay thanks. What I meant to say earlier is that I'm sorry about your wife. Not your life.

PETER: That's okay.

JANE JR.: My dad died when I was sixteen.

PETER: Yeah. I remember when that happened. Fucking brutal.

JANE JR.: Yeah.

PETER: Yeah. It all comes back brutal. Even the good stuff, you know? My wife she uh. She uh

JANE JR.: Yeah

PETER: She, yeah, she would get so goofy it was like she became a different person. Like a goofy noodle. Just noodling around the house like a goofy noodle. Sometimes it would confuse me because she'd do it when things were weird, when the mood was bad, like we'd just had a fight or something. And I would get mad sometimes, thinking she was trying to send a message, like saying she hated how sad I was. Which maybe she did. But now I'm thinking about her eyes when she did it, she really just *became* a goofy noodle. Like me and my sad bullshit—coming outta nowhere. She couldn't help it. Just the goofiest fucking noodle. And why didn't I laugh more at it?

(Pause.)

JANE JR.: It's okay if you don't want to, but I really liked that, and I'm wondering if you'll tell me another story?

(He looks at her, and then reaches into his pocket and takes out a small booklet—five pieces of paper stapled together.)

What's that?

PETER: It's my favorite story ever.

JANE JR.: Yes.

Read it.

PETER: "My daddy is a funny kid. His name is Peter Dad Oreos. Clak. He yells at a phone. Hivve? He works fo the snow. Once upon a time, was a dad. He hated about snow. Here is the truk, taller then a sky. The clouds are snow. The stars are salt. He climes forever. He scremms for us. The day was cold. But he got up and went outside. And I warm up. The end."

(Maiworm enters. She takes off her boots and hits the snow off them. She looks at her daughter.)

MAIWORM: Are you okay?

THE END

WILL ARBERY is a playwright and screenwriter. *Corsicana* premiered at Playwrights Horizons in 2022 and was a *New York Times* Critic's Pick. *Evanston Salt Costs Climbing* had its New York premiere at The New Group and was the subject of a feature in *The New York Times Magazine*. His play *Heroes of the Fourth Turning*, also available from TCG Books, premiered at Playwrights Horizons in 2019 and was a Pulitzer Prize Finalist, Obie winner, Lortel winner, and New York Drama Critics' Circle Award winner. It was named one of the best plays of the year by *The New York Times*, *Vulture*, *Time Out*, and more. Other plays include: *Plano* (Clubbed Thumb), *You Hateful Things* (NYTW Dartmouth Residency), and *Wheelchair* (3 Hole Press). He was the recipient of a Whiting Award in 2020. TV: *Succession* and *Irma Vep*. His work has been featured in *The Paris Review*. He's currently under commission from Manhattan Theatre Club, Adventureland, and The Metropolitan Opera. willarbery.com